Contents

tahiti
and its islands

text
Bob Putigny

photography
Mike Hosken • B. Hermann • M. Folco • C. Rives • E. Christian

"In order to preserve the glamour of this dreamland,
I should have allowed it to remain untouched.
For those around me have spoiled my Tahiti,
trying to explain it according to their own ways.
They are those who drag along their empty characters,
their down-to-earth ideas, everywhere they go,
soiling all poetry with their mockery,
their own insensibility and their foolishness.
And civilisation has come here too often —
all our conventions, our habits, our vices.
And this wild poetry fades away,
with all the manners and traditions of the past."

Pierre Loti

LES·EDITIONS·DU·PACIFIQUE

French Polynesia

At the heart of the vast Pacific, the single ocean that covers two thirds of the globe, lies jewel-like Tahiti. This evocative name is used to refer not only to the island of Tahiti itself, but the group of islands, including that one, which constitutes French Polynesia.

The islands are of two types: the *high islands* formed by volcanic activity, whose verdant peaks seem to spring out of the sea; and the *low islands* or *atolls*, palm-strewn coral rings that scarcely rise above sea level. They are concentrated in five archipelagos: the Windward Islands (Iles du Vent), Leeward Islands (Sous-le-Vent), which together are called the Society Islands, Tuamotu and Gambier, the Marquesas, and Austral, so far removed from one another that their total 4,000 km² of *terra firma* is scattered over an area greater than that of the European continent. At 9,000 km from Santiago and Tokyo, 7,000 km from San Francisco, 6,000 km from Sydney, 4,500 km from Honolulu, and 4,000 km from Auckland, Tahiti is at the crossroads of inter-island and intercontinental communications by sea and air.

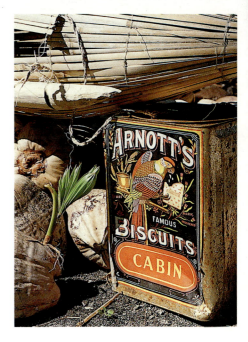

The isles of French Polynesia, protected by their barrier reefs from the moods of the ocean, are not known as "dream islands" for nothing. Pirogue teams train each evening between Tahiti and Moorea for the regularly scheduled races, hoping to bring glory to their clubs (preceding double page).
Lagoon and coconut trees (left) stand as symbols of the natural resources that work as man, the exploiter, relaxes. The little trap and its improvised float (above) bespeak the festive results of Tahitian-style fishing.

Climate

All the island groups of Polynesia boast a tropical climate, on the hot and humid side but tempered by the tradewinds. The year is divided into two seasons: from December to March it is especially warm and there is much rain, and from June to October is the cooler dry season. The temperature ranges over the course of a year from a low of 18° C to a high of 32° C. The water temperature is between 23° and 26° C. The high proportion of sunny to cloudy days has made it possible to use solar power to satisfy domestic energy needs to an exceptional extent.

Although French Polynesia lies outside the normal cyclone zone, it has not been totally free of these devastating storms. On at least two occasions in this century, the islands were subject to the winds' destructive forces: at the beginning of the century (1903-04) the Tuamotu Islands were hit very hard; and in 1982-83 storms caused considerable damage to Tahiti, but luckily few casualties resulted, thanks to the quick and precise instructions given the population.

The high islands, spent volcanoes, have broken contours providing superb bays, like those of Oponohu and Cook on Moorea (above, left, with Tahiti in the background). The low islands, or atolls, are rings cut by water-passes to the interior lagoons.

Airplanes (above) have made sister islands like Tahiti and Moorea no more than a "flea's jump" apart. Those that are further apart have been brought closer together by the advent of medium-range aircraft.

History

Bold navigators, furrowing the sea with their double pirogues, first arrived in eastern Polynesia from the west around 300 A.D., probably in the Marquesas, from which they flocked toward Hawaii, Easter Island and the Society Islands — or so, at any rate, it is currently understood; the scholarly view of how Polynesia was populated may change, as new archaeological evidence comes to light.

The European discoverer of the Marquesas was the Spaniard Mendaña, in 1595, and the Portuguese Queiros found the Tuamotu Islands in 1606. But it was an Englishman, Wallis, who was the first white man to land at Tahiti proper, aboard the *Dolphin*, in June 1767.

After Wallis' somewhat turbulent visit, Louis-Antoine de Bougainville "rediscovered" Tahiti in early April 1768 on his voyage around the world with the *Boudeuse* and *Etoile*. It was he, in a book written on his return, who instigated the myth of an island paradise on the basis of this first contact between Frenchman and what they called the "New Cythera". Captain Cook's turn came in 1769 when he stopped in Tahiti, at the site known now as Point Venus, to observe the transit of the planet Venus across the sun.

These sailors and the journals they kept contributed to a growing body of general mythology regarding these fortunate isles and their happy inhabitants, living free and ignorant of the constraints that weighed on the societies of old Europe. The European thinkers of the late 18th century — reflected by Rousseau's philosophy — took up the theme, and the whole continent began dreaming of Tahiti, the island in the Great Ocean where the Golden Age had never ended and the "noble savage" was not yet extinct.

The Tahitians possessed neither written language, nor metal, nor even the institution of work, but they had produced something that some people would value more: a happy civilisation. The agreeable climate helped, no doubt, and so did the environment's freedom from dangerous fauna and its wealth of natural resources — although these were actually less abundant then than they are now. Polynesian society was based on a rigid social hierarchy: chiefs and priests possessed powers of supernatural origin, and were not to be questioned. They wielded their authority through the *tapu*, or religious interdiction. The violation of a *tapu*, knowing or otherwise, was a crime that had to be punished.

Religious organization centred on the *marae*, a place and institution often mentioned in this book. Forum of the gods and spirits and their intermediaries, the *marae* was a ceremonial space that played a complex role in every aspect of social life, both spiritual and political. It is this system that gave Polynesian life "a harmony based on profound belief". It served both as a code of civil justice and as a police force in a world without prisons.

It would be naive to imagine that this was a world free of war, clan conflicts and dynastic quarrels. The "discoverers" from the other side of the world realized that and were not above exploiting it, even those of them who idealized Polynesian society the most, while local people on their part made use of the presence of foreigners for their own political purposes. But in their battles, in spite of brutality and cruelty, in spite of the fact that one side inevitably lost and the other won, at least they did not behave with the kind of

The past together with the beginnings of the modern era: top left, a bone tiki by one of the Marquesan master-craftsmen that produced these more ornamental than religious ivi polo; below left, a more ceremonial than functional (the ornamentation shows) paddle from the Australs.
Besides documents of a scientific character, like the botanical etchings on Cook's voyages by Parkinson, we have varied interpretations of Tahiti and the explorers' sojourns there in paintings and drawings. As captured in the engraving below, the delicate Tahitian light was flattering when Pomare II offered a meal to the Russian navigator Bellingshausen.

fanaticism that the old European peoples had developed, by those days, to such a pitch of bloody perfection.

Then, pell-mell, great sailors and great mutineers, traders and artists, whalers and scientists, soldiers and adventurers, businessmen and churchmen, began to congregate on the island, all profiting from its hospitality, many abusing its trust. In 1842, after long years of struggle between the great powers and between rival missionary groups, France established its protectorate over Tahiti during the reign of Pomare IV. The conflict did not end there: when Reverend Pritchard, an enemy of France, was named English Consul, Admiral Dupetit-Thouars had him arrested and expelled from Tahiti, the incident almost leading to further Anglo-French conflict. Tahitian unrest was reflected in domestic problems, including an insurrection, before King Pomare V accepted the joining of the Society Islands to France in an act signed into law June 29, 1880.

The ensuing era of the "Etablissements Français d'Océanie" was marked by the homesteading of colonists,

Below: the port of Papeete in 1877, in one of the precious watercolours by the "lady traveller" C.F. Cordon Cumming. The view, with Moorea in the background, is from the godown belonging to the Bramders, an English-originating family whose trading house was a great commercial power of the time. Right: nature's exuberance, in a watercolour by the Englishman G. Tobin.

French and Anglo-Saxon; by the development of a Chinese community starting out from workers recruited in 1864 for cotton cultivation; and by the evolution of a multi-ethnic society — more varied in some archipelagos than others — throughout the islands. Then, after World War II, in which Tahitians had been part of the Pacific Batallion that acquitted itself so gloriously at Bir Hakeim, came the age of "French Polynesia".

Starting in 1963, Polynesia entered yet another era with the installation of the Pacific Experimentation Centre (CEP), just two years after the total opening of the islands to the outside world with the inauguration of the international airport of Tahiti-Faaa. An intermediary political phase of internal self-management began in 1977, followed by statutory internal autonomy in 1984. A president, designated by the 41 members of the Territorial Assembly, heads the government for a five-year term. The French State is represented by a high commissioner of the Republic, while Polynesia is represented in France by two deputies and a senator.

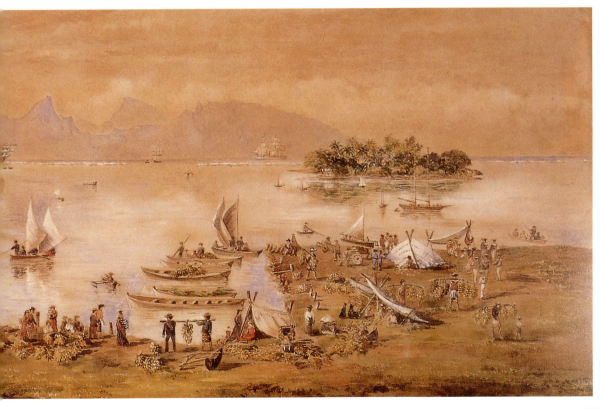

Flora and Fauna of the Islands

A vegetation of legendary profusion and variety is the traveller's inexhausible source of wonderment. But many of the species have been introduced from outside, especially in the Society Islands, like the frangipani (above) and the heliconia (above right) with its strange "false bird-of-paradise" blossoms. The tiare-tahiti (Gardenia Taitensis), a native, as delicate as it is fragrant, remains the symbol of the island (bottom right).

The distinctive Polynesian flora varies in beauty and diversity according to the latitude and type of the particular island on which it may be found.

Atolls, with their dry, calcareous soil, have a relatively poor flora. Apart from the ubiquitous coconut tree, there is only a scrub growth of *miki-miki*, along with pandanus and the occasional breadfruit tree or *maiore*; flowers — periwinkles and tiara gardenias — are rare indeed.

On the high islands like Tahiti itself, in contrast, rich soil and humidity encourage a greater diversity of trees and plants. Other than on the very high ground, which is covered with ferns and brushwood, the vegetation is remarkably varied, and its profusion is a delightful surprise to the visitor seeing it for the first time. In the cool damp valleys, *mape* (Tahitian chestnut tree), bamboos, *fei* (wild bananas), and pandanus grow; on the coast are the useful fruit trees, coconut, breadfruit, mango and banana. And above all there are flowers. Blending with the native Tahitian tiaras and *pua*, in a perpetual enchantment, are the yellow lianas, multicoloured clusters of royal poinciana, bougainvillea, hibiscus bushes, and crotons of all colours.

Fauna

In Tahiti, as on the other islands of French Polynesia, you find none of the amazing animals of tropical cliché; no monkeys mimicking human gestures or parrots imitating human speech. This may make them less romantic, and perhaps less profitable for the tourist trade. On the other hand, however, neither are there any poisonous or dangerous animals, except for outsize centipedes, whose stings cause a few hours' swelling, and mosquitos. The first Polynesian immigrants brought pigs, dogs and chickens along on their double pirogues; rats and lizards were aboard as stowaways.

Europeans have had some luck importing domestic animals including horses, cows, cats and turkeys, but not so with the Molucca mynah: it was brought in to control a wasp population that was devastating the fruit orchards, but found it more convenient to eat the fruits itself, so that as the mynahs proliferated and the wasps did not diminish, the fruit orchards suffered even greater damage.

Land birds, sea birds and migratories from Asia, Africa, Australia and America have made their way from island to island, finding and adapting to suitable niches in the immense Polynesian territory. But on Tahiti, the sea birds — so useful to fishermen in locating shoals of fish — are now becoming rare; the ever-increasing concentration of human population along the coast has limited the birds' habitat. The most prolific, most varied, and most interesting, species make their homes in the woodlands.

Tahiti must now consider the question of protecting its precious, gracious, delicate endowment of nature: roadwork, earthworks, intense traffic may be necessary for development, but they raise problems for an environment all the more precious in the limitations of island space. Here more than elsewhere, the maintenance of a natural equilibrium will depend on an intelligent mastery of technology.

Many of the birds of Polynesia — the local nesters and migratories alike — need vigilant protection. From left to right and from top to bottom: the revered Tahitian kingfisher, which haunts the valleys of the Societies; the swift tern, which hardly leaves the reef; the great frigatebird, common throughout Polynesia; the "holy egret" or reef heron, a familiar sight of beaches and rivers; the Tahiti flycatcher, to be seen only on that island, and only in medium altitude forest; and the lesser golden plovers, who winter in Polynesia, with one of the wandering tattlers that explore the upriver areas.

Underwater Fauna

The exceptionally rich underwater world of the lagoons offers the amateur marine biologist an infinity of surprises. All that is asked is that collectors moderate their delight with respect for the delicate ecological balance. There are still plenty of cowries (above) of admirable colour and sheen, but the same cannot be said for tritons and conchs (right), now becoming rare.

Polynesia possesses some of the most varied underwater life in the world. The diversity of species evolving in these waters and the endless beauty of the setting provide much material for wonder to aqua-nautical enthusiasts from the sporting diver and fisherman to the discerning shell-collector and underwater photographer.

In their intricate coral branchworks or on the sandy floors surrounding them, the reefs hide a multicoloured riot of sea urchins, rainbows of elegantly — and exotically — shaped shells, langoustes (or lobsters), crabs and giant clams. Within or beyond the reef, however, it is the fish that are the most diverse, creating their own carnival of hues, their own menagerie of shape and style. The shark, though less belligerent than its Australian cousin, is the undisputed sovereign of Polynesian waters. Sedentary bass and grouper stay close to the reef with their neighbours, snapper, sea perch, and the surgeonfish with its lancet-like spines. Parrotfish and wrasse prefer to travel in shoals, while the moray eel guards the mouths of corals caverns.

Shells

Molluscs come a close second to fish in the list of attractions of the underwater world. The reefs and lagoons offer a vast variety of different environments, adapted to an enormous number of different species.

Although collectors may be ecstatic over the shellfish, they must take care that, while on the hunt, they do not contribute to the destruction of the coral ecosystem that the shells require for growth and reproduction. Beyond their aesthetic value, the shells are intrinsically important to the islands' economy as well. Mother-of-pearl, once collected for the nacre alone, is now used for sophisticated pearl culture as well. The troca shell, brought into Polynesia in 1957, is harvested by the ton in its short annual fishing season, eventually to be crafted into curios, buttons, accessories and other small nacre objects.

Lastly, shells are a kind of symbol of the region, as it is traditional to give departing guests a shell necklace as a farewell gift. Such a necklace will draw them to return one day to the islands' enchanted shores.

The diversity of colours and whimsicality of forms of the lagoon fish are a source of wonder. Among them are (top left to right) the chameleon sea bass (hoa), zebra surgeonfish (maroa), burnt parrotfish (paati paapaa auahi), yellow angelfish (oaragaraga) and "coachman fish" (paraha tore). On the other side of this reef-protected universe prowls one of the lords of the underwater jungle, a black-finned shark, always in search of prey.

Tahiti

"On the third of June 1767, we saw a large number of seagulls, which together with the uncertainty of the weather made us hope that we were nearing land. The next day a tortoise swam clear up to the vessel. The fifth, we took note of several birds, which confirmed us in the hope of finding a landfall. On the sixth, at 11:00 in the morning, a sailor called Jonathan Puller cried from the maintop, 'Land west by northwest!' By noon it could be seen distinctly from the deck, a low island around five or six leagues away. The joy felt by all of us upon this discovery cannot be imagined by those who have never experienced the dangers, fatigues and sorrows of a voyage like that which we had made."

– Samuel Wallis

"The appearance of this coast, raised into the shape of an amphitheatre, was a most cheerful sight. Although the mountains are very high, one sees no bare arid rock; all is forested over." – L.-A. de Bougainville

Few people, alas, have the opportunity to discover Tahiti by sea nowadays. In most cases, it is from one of the long-haul flights that unload cargoes of travel-worn tourists daily at Tahiti-Faaa International airport.

The view as one comes in by air is striking all the same: Moorea in the foreground, Tahiti behind, upon a field of the ocean's dark blue and the white foam of the reef's edge, the whole complemented by the myriad greens of the lagoon and the sombre mass of mountains hung with clouds, creating an altogether memorable image.

An aerial view of the Windward Islands suggests the inevitable adaptation of a way of life to the constraints determined by geography. The island's ancient volcanic mass becomes an impregnable fortress, as the plane descends towards it. The rest of the island describes a narrow-looking circlet of land skirting the volcanic crest. The concentration of inhabitants on this ring of amenable soil explains the bustling social energy to be found there. Even though it is possible, before landing, to descry a ladder of habitations climbing the foothills to the heights of the capital, Papeete, the island people turn essentially toward the sea, toward the lagoon and its serenity, something of which the newcomer is very soon aware.

For air passengers, the first sign of Tahiti is that of a volcanic mountain range. Once aground, they take the colourful shore road, but the mountain still dominates whenever they raise their eyes. It is a jagged, violent elevation from the sharp teeth of Diadem (1330 m) to the peaks and needles of Orohena (2241 m), Pito Iti (2110 m) and Aoria (2066 m). Throughout the interior, there are valleys, opened to the littoral by the broad mirrors of freshwater estuaries where Tahitians love to swim.

Papeete

The capital of French Polynesia, with a population of almost 60,000 counting concentrations in the suburbs, lies on the northwest coast of Tahiti Island, between the highlands and a well set-up port. Papeete is the site of the High Commission of French Polynesia, the Territorial Assembly and the Government, the location of banks, travel agencies, the Tourist Office, the post office, department stores and Chinese shops, hotels, cinemas, night clubs, two hospitals and a host of restaurants, European as well as Chinese.

Since the construction of an international-class airport and the installation of the Pacific Experimentation Centre, the shape of the capital has been completely transformed. The little tropical town the size of a French provincial sub-prefecture, with its quiet shady streets and the backwater charm of its colonial-style houses, has given way to a glass and concrete city choked with noisy traffic, glared upon by street lights, consumed by an encroachment of asphalt park-

Nowadays, on the Papeete seafront, little steamboats have replaced the old schooners that used to service the Windward Islands. But the seafront really belongs to the fishermen with their "bonito-boats", available to organize fishing parties for angling tourists. Sailboats and yachts line up democratically deck to deck as if ready to race to other horizons — unless it is here that the goal of their voyage lies.

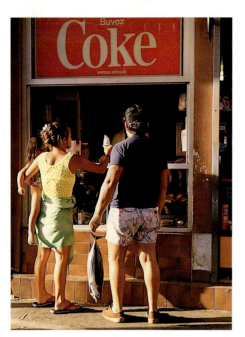

ing lots. Trees have been replaced by streetlamps, lawns by cement, and neon lights up the night sky instead of the stars. The people of Tahiti have got used to tourism; as the money economy sucks them in a proletariat is coming into existence. The easy, dreamy life has gone in favour of the nine-to-five, the political game and the deal: "You can't stop progress," as they say. But along the quays, yachts from all over the world, even as they prove Papeete to be a switch-yard of the Pacific, still symbolize a great escape.

The Market

Jolly ambience; the floor constantly washed down with vast quantities of water; not a single bad smell; gleaming fish, pyramids of papayas, watermelons, mangoes, fruits of every kind; the market is not only the "belly" of Papeete, but its heart as well. This is the preferred meeting place of Polynesians from all the islands and the point of origin of half the stories that travel down the "coconut-tree tele-

graph". Its moments of greatest animation come when the fish arrives, usually at 5:00 in the morning and 4:00 in the afternoon. The profusion of fruits and vegetables which greets the visitor might represent a week's or a month's harvest to a farmer from one of the nearby islands, and he will not go home until it is all sold. In Papeete, he will stay either with relatives or in the covered hall beside the market. Every evening, the building turns into a minicipal dormitory where anyone can lay out his mat and move in.

The waking of all these voluntary exiles is the occasion for a good deal of regularised bustle: they get up, wash, and finish the morning's rite in one of the cafés that surround the market, starting the day with a black coffee accompanied by the local beignets, *firi-firi*. By 4 or 5 a.m. the merchants from the local districts have arrived on *les trucks*, the local buses, and the market is open for business, though not, here, of the shrieking and haggling sort: the exuberance is especially in the colour, the phosphorescences of the fish and the velvets of fruits and flowers.

The active and the indolent alike crowd the streets of Papeete. Department store windows have not distracted people from the multitude of small traders, shops where one can get a quick drink and a beignet, *little tables selling lottery tickets, meeting places where two Vespas stop while their owners,* fetii *(friendly cousins), exchange greetings, gossip and smiles.*

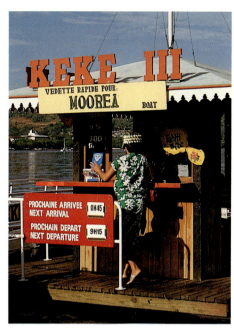

There are several connections per day between Tahiti and Moorea, by ferry and motorboat. The crossing of between half an hour and an hour is quick, and familiar to most of the users. The dock area is a highly animated scene as a strange assortment of merchandise piles up under the eyes of tourists awaiting their trip to the neighbouring island.

"Eaha ta oe ohipa i rira mama ruau?"
"Te tiai ra vau ia mahiti te fare tinito, isa roa ite punu ahu e hoi vau na niiho ite pereo ma-tainaa..."
"Eo Teva aita ona i haere mai ite oire na muriho ia oe?"
"Ua faea tu o Teva i Papara, e haere hoi ona ite haapiiraa..."

"What are you doing there, grandmother?"
"I'm waiting for the Chinese man to open his shop, and after I've bought my basin I'm going back to the truck."
"And Teva didn't come into town with you?"
"Teva? No, he stayed in Papara, it's a school day, you know..."

The *Vahine*

The *vahine* in the romantic sense, the ideal of the Tahitian woman that has served as the island's trademark for so long, is now a thing of the past. It is two centuries since Bougainville wrote, *en connaisseur*, "They yield nothing to most European women in the charm of their faces, and would outshine any of them as far as beauty of the body is concerned.... If Venus is goddess of love, here she is also goddess of hospitality, and her worship allows no mystery: the pleasure of love is public in a way our customs have forbidden...." The girls of the New Cythera used to swim around newly arrived ships, enchanting the sailors with proffered flowers and caresses. But this cannot be arranged for the tens of thousands of tourists spilling out of jets each year. The island has become virtuous; the delicious species of Bougainville's time seems to have gone the way of the sirens and fairies. Today, you can find the face of Rarahu, from the Pierre Loti novel, or Gauguin's model Tehura,

The retail trade in Tahiti can work out of a small handmade basket or a modern complex like that of Vaima (below right), bringing together store, luxury boutiques and travel agencies. Another gathering place, also along the seafront, is the post office (below), with its tropical architectural flavour, and one of the many brightly-coloured les trucks *that ply the island.*

working in a bank, or an import-export house. Admirable features and sumptuous figures delight the eye in the street, in the shops, in the residential areas: a torso and shoulders of sovereign splendour, a sublimely-shaped back narrowing to slender hips on legs as round as the columns of an Athenian temple. A marvelous balance in the way she walks, and also in the way she sees things as floating hair frames eyes with an expression of incalculable depth. Gauguin spoke of "the gold of their bodies", a polished-amber skin of unexpected, heart-rending softness.

Tahitians

Bougainville claimed that he had never run across better-built or better-proportioned men: "A painter could find no better models anywhere for Mars or Hercules." Philibert de Commerson spoke of the women as "rivals in beauty of the women of Georgia and, naked, sisters of the Graces themselves." Put less poetically, they have full shoulders, flat

and muscled backs, round thighs and big feet, which give them their superb balance. Their skin is particularly fine, their black hair thick and heavy, the mouth fleshy and beautifully shaped. Their eyes are often set rather far apart, putting an emphasis on the emotions they express, which can pass from joy to sorrow suddenly, without transition, or become altogether lost beyond the material world. Disoriented every now and then by the contradictions and complications of modern life, on the whole they look at things with a certain fatalism. They do not tend to take an attitude of aggression, or open scorn, to the "civilisation" of the *popaa*, or white-skinned invaders: astonishment, rather, compounded of ironic detachment and the feeling that the *popaa* are not altogether comprehensible; the sense of belonging still to a lost world that was both simpler and better, and yet a world they can still reach, intermittently, in the exaltation of a festive *bringue*.

Tahitians have a novel notion of life. To them, time, free time, is real wealth, and work is seen not as a way of

At night, which falls early in these latitudes, Papeete's active life spills out along the seafront and the adjacent streets. Cinemas, restaurants and brasseries beckon to idlers who have not left the city for the green districts. Vans equipped with bar and kitchen ensure the possibility of a meal à-l'improviste, and a feeling of the picturesque, on the quays, looking out at the twinkling lights of the port.

producing wealth, but as a sacrifice one has to make to one's permanent needs — one reason why the colonizers have made some attempt to create artificial needs for them.

And yet, in the age of communication satellites, no one can remain indifferent to events that concern every inhabitant of the planet. With the advent of the video who can resist the pleasure of watching a film for one's favourite star? And how could they have remained unelectrified, given the possibility of solar power? The more remote the island, the more pleased the people are with their progress. But modernization seems to imply a dull-minded pursuit of "resource creation" which may not be compatible with Tahitians' lack of pettiness and serious aptitude for pleasure.

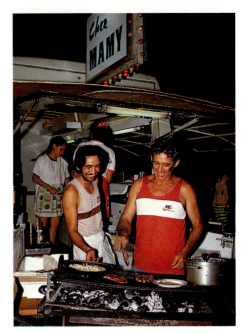

It is to be hoped that the Polynesian cultural genius can prove itself in finding a way to reconcile tradition and modernism, protecting the roots of the one as it harvests the fruits of the other, giving justice to Bougainville's words, written in the melancholy of departure, "Farewell, you wise and happy people! May you always be what you are."

However much it may transform and modernize itself, Papeete's market keeps its multicoloured charm intact. The flower vendors start offering early in the morning, the wicker baskets of lemon, banana, grapefruit, mango, and the shell necklaces as well; you can see the weighing of a tuna that promises much pleasure to the person who buys it, or the smile of a delighted child, fresh from a family fishing trip, watching the hungry buyers. All this amid interrogations and laughter, while a convoy of les trucks from all the municipalities of the island chases its tail.

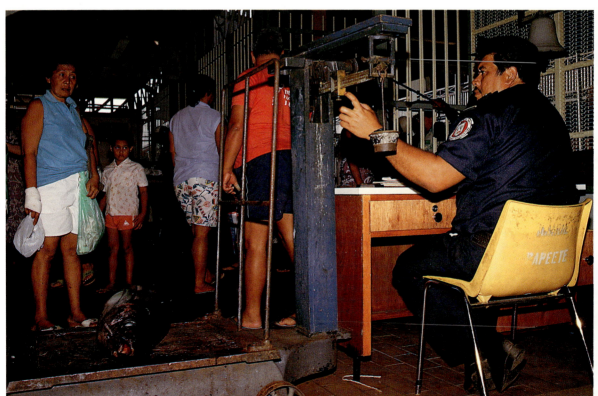

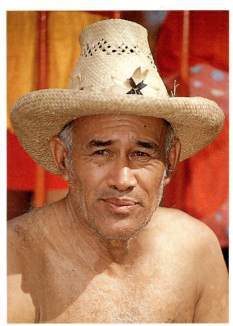

Whether in a gorgeously laid out Papeete store or a rustic shop on the shore road, the grocer always seems to be a Tahitian Chinese. "Metropolitan", that is French, brands sit next to New Zealand lamb and butter, home-grown fruits and vegetables and the local papers. When, occasionally, Chinese add baking to the list of their functions, it means a crispy, tasty loaf of exquisite quality.

The fish of the open sea and of the lagoon as
well are eaten poached and barbecued, but especially raw. To prepare raw fish (facing page),
take a bonito, tuna or parrotfish, skin, fillet and
cut up the flesh into cubes. Marinate in salt and
fresh-squeezed lemon juice for ten minutes,
then pour off some of the liquid, add raw vegetables and coconut milk and serve chilled.
Another way, called fafaru, is to cover the fish
with sea water in a calabash and let it sit for
two or three days, then pour the juice onto diced
pieces of fresh fish, marinating for at least six
hours, according to taste.

Sport

Given an unusually youthful and vigorous population, Tahiti is naturally devoted to a variety of sports, as the construction and maintenance of more and more stadiums shows. Football [or "soccer"] is quite popular, originally played barefoot, but rapid progress has been made so there are hopes now of reaching the international level. Boxing holds an important place in the list of local sports because, for the Polynesian public, it is the embodiment of the values of expressiveness and defiance.

Depending on the season and the direction of the wind, the long waves of Papara and Papenoo offer splendid opportunities for surfing, which is of course the original Polynesian sport. Joseph Banks, the English naturalist who accompanied Captain Cook, credited the Tahitians with inventing it, writing: "Their favourite play is to push floating before them, an old pirogue, to look for the most distant wave and then to leap quickly, sometimes two at a time, upon it and

Bridges cross rivers at several points on the road around the island. This is the place for the favourite break for children and adults alike, a swim in the fresh flowing water at the end of the day. At km 41 of the west-coast highway, the plain of Altimaono is the setting for one of the most beautiful golf courses in the South Pacific.

then, with the most tapered end facing the breaking wave, their agility lets them be carried at an incredible speed, sometimes clear to the shore…".

Considering the islands and their surroundings, all water sports are naturally popular. Not surprisingly, Polynesian culture sets a high value on playing sport for pleasure, but not on sport for business purposes, or the lonely working out of a neurotic, competitive or personal obsession, which has led some Western observers to consider Tahitian athetes "undisciplined" and "unprofessional." But games that join a community to the joys of reflex action and skill, especially volleyball and basketball, appeal to islanders' natural proclivities and have ever more numerous advocates. Accordingly, the most exalting sight in Tahiti, perhaps, is that of a pirogue race, where people who have been sailors virtually since birth display knowledge and endurance of an international class. If this sport ever becomes part of the Olympics, it is a safe bet that the Tahitians will find a place on the podium.

Dances

Dancing is the most natural and spontaneous form of Tahitian expression. Tahitians are never tired or bored with dancing, never *fiu*, or fed up. When someone strikes up the frenetic rhythm of the wooden *toere* drums, whether it is in a Papeete street or the remotest corner of the districts, all men and women, children and old people, rush out in a single movement to observe and criticise the dancing — which can be seen several times a day and night — without any diminishment of enthusiasm.

The *otea* is a dance of military origin, performed with wild power and speed. The *aparima* is performed from a seated position, lascivious and languid. The *paoa* is satirical, accompanied by a syncopated rhythm of drums and handclaps. *Ori-tahiti* or *tamure*, finally, matches scissor-steps for the men with shuddering gestures for the women, miming the act of love expressively enough to be fairly disconcerting for the unsophisticated foreign guest.

At the celebrations of Internal Autonomy and Tiurai, exotic competitions take place in Tahiti: spear-throwing at the target of a coconut 15 metres in the air, coconut-shelling, and above all this race of fruit carriers, running with a burden that must also be attractively presented.

Heiva I Tahiti

The successful assault on a disused fortress on July 14, 1789 in Paris, which signalled the beginning of the French Revolution, understandably had little immediate effect on Polynesian life. Since Tahiti became *French* Polynesia, however, the Polynesians have found Bastille Day to be a superb occasion for a complex of celebrations and festivities known collectively as *Tiurai*.

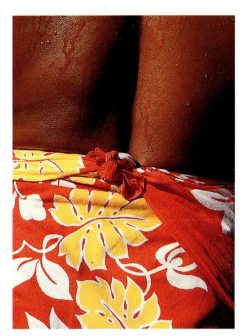

Over the years, *Tiurai* has gradually extended itself to encompass the entire month of July, including among its activities: races for everything from horses and pirogues to fruit carriers; other athletic competitions in archery and javelin-throwing; singing, dancing and coconut-husking contests; and the requisite food-hawkers and drinks.

Meanwhile, the statute of internal autonomy for French Polynesia, or *Heiva I Tahiti*, from 1985 is celebrated on June 29: so that now *Heiva I Tahiti* signals the beginning of the traditional *Tiurai* festivities.

Tour Around the Island

Tahitians scorn machinery in general, but they are mad about cars, and so the island contains an extraodinary number of them, whose power is only equalled by their uselessness on a beltroad where the speed limit is a chaste 70 km/hr. But the cars, and the occasions made for their use, are one of the local forms of snobbery: invariably the size of the cars is inversely proportionate to that of the island, and supposed to be directly related to the importance of the owner, much as in other recently mechanized societies. Every Sunday the inhabitants, on other islands of French Polynesia as well as Tahiti, take to their cars, as the circular highway becomes a shining carousel where mopeds, scooters, motorcycles, *les trucks* and all sorts of automobiles careen excitedly in a mad race around the island.

Polynesia's traditional Sunday drive around the perimeter of the island also serves as a good introduction to the Tahitian landscape for the tourist. Its 120 kilometres are normally taken in a clockwise direction. At the km 4 mark out of Papeete, heading northwest, is Arue, a fief of the royal dynasty, where the tomb of Tahiti's last king, Pomare V, is to be found at the seaside, with those of his ancestors and family. The hill of Taharaa affords an outstanding double-panoramic view, with the silhouette of Moorea in the background on one side, and the harmonious curve of Matavai ("Water-face") Bay on the other, with the coconut grove of Point Venus jutting into the sea. Point Venus itself, at km 10, which acquired its name from Captain Cook, was where most of the earliest European sailors all landed, except for Bougainville. He was fated to leave a number of anchors farther east, at Hitiaa.

After the Blow-Hole of Tiarei at km 22 — a rock formation through which the waves send a jet of water that can spurt as far as the road, sprinkling the unwary — there is a side road climbing the superb valley of Faarumai, a lush two kilometres of exuberent primeval vegetation. The dull roar of three waterfalls is impressive; one can imagine oneself in the Edenic gardens described so lovingly by Bougainville. Indeed, Hitiaa, where the great explorer landed in 1768, is hard by at km 39, the landing commemorated with a bronze plaque. At km 42 is the cascade of Faatautia, visible from the road, and then one arrives at Taiarapu Peninsula, km 55. This, too, can be visited, but only on foot or by boat.

A cluster of bananas, symbolizing the maximum nourishment for the minimum of effort. The development of kitchen gardening (left) evokes the picture of a different kind of work, patient and meticulous, that supplies the population of today with locally-grown lettuce, cabbage, eggplant, tomato and zucchini.

On the return to Papeete, the wild and grandiose east coast is left behind for the sheltered, flowery west. The port region of Phaeton is followed by the flower district of Papeari, at km 49.5, after which the road crosses the lush botanical gardens created 50 years ago by Harrison Smith. Atimaono's 18-hole golf course comes at km 40 on the road back, and then there are two *marae* structures (the *marae* being the communal focal point of Southeast Polynesian and Maori social, political and religious life): one by the sea at Mahaiatea (km 39), which is the largest in all Polynesia, unfortunately now in a sadly dilapidated state; and, after the Marra Cave (km 28.5), *marae* Arahurahu in a valley in Paea (km 22.5), very skillfully reconstructed by the Society of Oceania Studies. Across the residential neighbourhood of Punaauia, where the Maeva Hotel is located, at km 8, one gets back to Papeete either via the Faaa road, through the international airport, or directly via the RDO (Route de Dégagement Ouest) highway. Not that speeding is recommended there, either.

Tahitians may prefer fresh water bathing, in the river or under the spray of a waterfall, but they have a great fondness for the beach, where the ancestral practise of surfing has been revitalized by new surfboard techonology.

Beliefs

The ancient Polynesian mythology evidenced indisputable imaginative power and poetic sensibility, reflecting perhaps the inspirational lushness and beauty of the islandscape. The Polynesians' sacred or legendary tales, and their traditional knowledge, were maintained by priests who enjoyed great authority and prestige in ancient, pre-Christian Polynesian society. The Polynesians believed in an immortal soul and held that after physical death they would either participate in the delights of their paradise, *te havaiki*, or be reincarnated as creatures of the earth, sea or sky. They worshipped Taaroa, a creator deity who was the origin of all awareness and power, as well as secondary gods which included his children.

Religious ceremonies generally took place in a cleared, square space, the traditional *marae*. Enclosed by rough-cut stone or coral-slab walls, depending on the materials available on the individual island, the whole converged upon an

altar of piled stones at one end. It was upon this altar that the divine effigies were consecrated, and there the occasional human sacrifice would also be held.

This venerable religion has crumbled along with the stones of the *marae*, and the socio-political structure that sustained both. Polynesians have remained profoundly religious, but in a context of Christian belief, and now the majority in Tahiti and the Windwards are Protestant, in Tuamotu and the Marquesas Catholic, reflecting perhaps the religions of the islands' respective discoverers. Accordingly, they think of the Bible, in the translation of King Pomare II, as the only authentic Tahitian book. All evince great respect for the moral teachings of Christianity and, although they cannot bring themselves to consider physical love as a source of sin, they are naturally charitable, and never take the name of the Lord in vain. As for their assiduously attended church services, the magnificent chants, mostly drawn from traditional music of the islands, give the sacred offices an unusual emotional power.

Valleys open onto the Tahiti coast, all round the island. Pleasant and easy to enter, they beckon the traveller in. This valley (below) becomes rather more of an endurance test the further the explorer penetrates. Once inhabited and then abandoned, they are becoming popular again, thanks to the coastal population density and promises of refreshing riverside coolness.

Religious services emphasise choral singing and chanting. Evangelical churches (across, the Pao Fai church in Papeete) are especially attached to the traditional forms, helping sustain a Polynesian social and cultural identity, as services and Sunday school bring many worshippers to the churches. Mixing piety, great musical skill and the pleasures of belonging, Polynesian choral music has a sincere beauty.

Large choirs, or himene, *each having its own headgear and costume, represent districts, villages or associations. All achieve the same fervour and polyphonic tradition in which the rhythm, the echo of the basses and the nasal tones are entrancing. Opposite, the* himene *group of Mataiea. The* himene tarava *groups, of six to ten voices, attract big audiences.*

Songs

Singing punctuates all of Polynesian existence; there are songs for and at every occasion or situation; for religious ceremonies, feasts, burials, organized conferences and chance meetings; in the *bringues*, of course; and on journeys by land and sea. Wherever the place, whatever the occasion, the moment a group forms, it seems, a song surges from it, with or without accompaniment, as if celebrating a singular tradition with a single voice using bits of Polynesian folklore, or current hits, with Tahitian words tacked onto the latest tune from America or Europe.

With or without instrumental accompaniment or dancing, Tahitian songs are generally performed in harmonic chorus, sometimes embellished by solo parts.

Large choirs are known as *himene*. Many of the songs they perform are of ancient provenance: old Polynesia was pre-literate, and these songs were a significant part of the oral tradition through which Polynesian culture and identity

Any occasion — such as this gathering of youthful friends — is cause for celebration through music and song. Nowadays, the Tahitian musical and social traditions are supplemented with modern conveniences, including a portable stereo, broadcasting the latest music from Europe or America.

were preserved. There are the *tarava* telling of mighty historical or legendary deeds, others of a mainly religious character, and then the *fango*, the *paumotu* death songs, enchanting and tragic: the men, using cupped hands over their mouths as megaphones, cry in a hoarse monotone as they sway back to front, while the women play out a litany with a recurring cadence, a prolonged low falling tone like a dying breath. In the *ute*, a group of men and women sings a rhythmic refrain in throaty voices, while the comical or satirical verse is improvised by a soloist. Then there are the requisite songs of love, adventure and war, especially the *aparima*, *hivinau*, and *paoa*, taken up by the chorus in the course of a dance.

The *Bringue*

Pronounce it "brrrin-gue", with the characteristic, irreplaceable sound of the islands, where the French *r* rolls like pebbles in the rapids, and transforms the old argot term for

The Gauguin Museum in Papeari, with a world wide cultural reputation for its liveliness, presents the stages of the painter's life, his study, and sources of inspiration (above right, Contes Barbares [Barbarian Tales], Marquesas, 1902 from the Folkwang Museum, Essen). Below, an evocation of the painter's studio.

easting into a word for the Tahitian initiate, evoking guitars, bottles of beer, and garlands of flowers.

Much as is the case with Tahitian singing, any occasion can and will serve as an excuse for a *bringue* with one's family and friends: weddings, official holidays, private celebrations, the Saturday night round of Papeete's innumerable nightclubs and bars or the traditional Sunday morning drive around the island. In a world altered by modern concerns and conveniences, it is a well of renewal from which the Tahitian draws immense strength and enthusiasm for the return to everyday life.

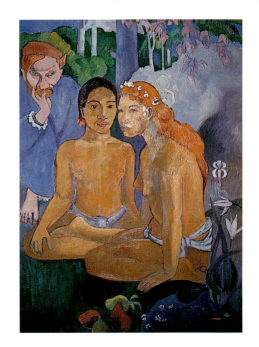

Art in Tahiti

Stifled by Parisian culture, the French painter Paul Gauguin found a new inspiration in the still-popular perception of an island paradise in the Pacific. Over his ten years in Tahiti and the Marquesas, where he lies buried, he made a new life and a new art. A museum in Papeari, built by the

Singer-Polignac Foundation, evokes his life and art in Tahiti. This, the Gauguin Museum, was donated to the Territory of French Polynesia in 1983, and now the Territory, in association with the Friends of the Gauguin Museum, manages its upkeep and development. Upwards of 50,000 people visit the museum each year, which exhibits paintings, sculptures, ceramics and prints by the painter, as well as works by his associates of the Pont-Aven school. Additionally, there is a historical section tracing Gauguin's life and his artistic sources in Oceanic art and mythology. But, perversely, much of the inspiration, Polynesian art itself, sacred sites, sculptures, even objects for daily use, have been destroyed.

However, there is now another museum, the Museum of Tahiti and its Islands, on the Pointe des Pecheurs in Punaauia, which is devoted to Polynesian culture. The history of the South Pacific is presented through archaeological exhibits; the natural environment, which is after all, so important to Polynesian civilisation is also there, in actual samples, photography, and audiovisual facilities.

The concept of the surfboard is at least as old as Polynesia. For very young afficionados it consists of anything that comes to hand, as long as it is flat and lightweight, but as they get older their developing skills justify the expense of going for more specialised materials. Very different from that vigorous amusement is the perspective of a picnic on the motu, with its tuft of coconut palms standing in the middle of the lagoon — the perfect image of the happiness of living beneath this kind of sky.

Where the barrier of the reef has a wide enough break in it, the power of the ocean pounds the beach directly. The curl of the wave is the surfer's joy, and the spray reminds some of sea-scapes from other hemispheres, especially on the east coast where there is no reef at all over considerable distances. It makes a striking contrast with the calm of the lagoon, to the appreciation of the crested tern, a bird that likes to turn its back on the great world to perch on anything sticking out of the water.

Moorea

The lacy silhouette of Tahiti's twin sister stretches out on the horizon 20 kilometres to the west of the main island, complementing and completing the prospect. Moorea: smaller, wilder, better preserved from "civilisation".

In reality, with electricity, television, and its own belt road for Sunday morning, Moorea no longer has anything to envy the big island across the way, and in fact may itself be envied; especially since it has managed to conserve its rural atmosphere, retaining a provincial charm evoked by some fine houses in local style, with palm or pandanus roofs.

With a runway for airplanes, Moorea is a mere seven minutes from Tahiti-Faaa, and traffic between the two goes on more or less continuously from dawn to dusk. But the sea crossing is one of those special moments which really would be a shame to miss just to save a little time: the view of the approach to Moorea, before the pass of Pao Pao Bay, is one of the finest sights Polynesia, perhaps the planet, can offer.

Two bays cut into the north coast of Moorea: Pao Pao, or Cook's Bay, so called because the famous explorer stayed there, and Opunohu. These two hollows, abrupt tropical "fjords", with their contrasts of light and diversity of colours, the sharp contorted shapes of the rocks and vegetation, make for an unusually splendid landscape.

Because Moorea has one of the loveliest lagoons in the Society Islands, the need for vigilance in safeguarding its ecological balance cannot be too strongly emphasized, menaced as it is by the negligence of inhabitants and careless visitors alike. Protecting the lagoon means protecting the entire ecosystem, its banks and bottoms, its coral and other fauna, all of which contribute to its grace and beauty. No one can fail to realize this, in the face of the incomparable variety of blues and greens at play in the light, and the iridescent clarity of the water along the fine sand beaches.

The 60 km road around the island leads, taking the airport as a starting point, to Afereaitu, Maatea, and Haapiti with its old church dating back to the first missionaries. Coming back toward the northwest brings you to the busier area, where the installation of hotels has brought about a population concentration. The Motu Fareone islets front the village of Club Med, situated along a sumptuous white

Many are the city-dwellers of Papeete whose favourite weekend escape is Moorea. If Tahiti is somewhat short of sand beaches, Moorea is very long on them. Coconut and iron trees spread shade over the hot blond sand in a setting where dreams of paradise meet with an altogether natural reality.

Fish are here, as everywhere in Polynesia, like an astrological sign of the place, and all the gourmet buyer need worry about is when to say "enough". The silhouette of Moorea, opposite, shows Mt. Tohivea (1207 m) dominating the chiselled ridge between the bays. The names of the peaks are associated with legends: Moua-puta, the "pierced rock", is said to have been the site of a battle between the champion Pai and Hiro, the god of thieves. Rotui, the trail souls follow on their way to the afterlife, saw the anquish of the giant Tafai searching for the spirit of his dead wife.

beach. The Club itself is one of the successes of its genre — in the "pseudo-Polynesian" style, harmonizing with its surroundings and melting into the landscape, despite its 350 rooms. And the usual activities predominate: tennis, water-skiing, scuba diving, pirogues, glass-bottomed boats, and of course performances of Tahitian song and dance at the gentle members' pleasure.

Afterwards, on the way to Papetoai, there is a little chapel with a Pierre Heyman painting to admire, then the bay of Opunohu, and from there a road to the grounds of the School of Agriculture and the lookout pavilion atop Mount Tohivea. Agriculture plays an essential part in Moorea's economy, and the island was in fact a former capital of vanilla cultivation. It is now dominated by market-garden cultivation of fruits and flowers, especially pineapple, which is successful enough in quality and quantity that the island now has its own fruit juice factory.

Looping the loop along the bay of Pao Pao, you return to the airfield by Maharepa, after passing through the main

tourist district, with its charming hotels of bungalows on stilts. The countryside revealed on this little periplus is something quite different from what is found on Tahiti.

For one thing, the landscape is more open, less boxed off; instead of hedges, the homesteads are divided by dishevelled rows of *riri*, a kind of lily with bright green leaves that rarely grows higher than a metre, so that it is easy to see the *fare* ("house") hemmed around by hibiscus and tropical gardenia, banana groves, and here and there an old home from the gilded era of vanilla.

Lastly, Moorea, once known as Aimeho, is rich in archaeological relics, *marae*, platforms for archery, terraces for dwellings. The reconstructed *marae* of Opunohu and Afareaitu, the splendour of the sites, a kind of atmosphere of the old-fashioned that marks all the coastal villages, all these allow the visitor to understand the original character of an island and its inhabitants: so near to a modern, if modest, capital of the Pacific, Moorea owed it to itself to preserve the noble charm of a long history.

In a hurry, passage by air between Tahiti and Moorea is no more than a flea-jump. Those who know how to live, however, will take one of the boats. Anyone who has anything to transport, which is to say everyone who lives here, will make use of the trucks and vans to bring home the packages that have sailed from Papeete, unless they load their own Vespas, which have replaced what was once the ideal mode of transport in Moorea, the horse.

The Leeward Islands

"In spite of the tropical vegetation, the lines of this landscape are so pure and the light so delicate that there is something Anacreontic about it."   – A. t'Serstevens

Northwest of Moorea and Tahiti are the "Iles-Sous-le-Vent", as the French call them, or Leeward Islands, because one sails for them against the prevailing tradewinds from the north-northwest. They consist of five islands and four atolls, the latter being isolated in the open sea and not frequently visited.

Geographically, Huahine, Raitea and Tahaa, Bora Bora and Maupiti form a kind of extension to the Society Archipelago as Cook "discovered" it in 1769. Their total surface area of about 400 km² is modest in comparison to that of Tahiti, which surpasses 1,000 km² on its own. The disproportion in sizes is not the only thing that makes Tahiti seem like a mainland to the islands; it is also the fact that Tahiti has Papeete, the administrative, commercial and financial switchyard of the Territory.

All the same, though the Leewards may be mere vassals of Papeete, it is far from difficult to find an especially charming Polynesia in them: there is some degree of a fixed local life, a particular rhythm and characteristic activities.

The airplane has put the Leeward Islands at a short time-distance from Tahiti, but all of them are still between two to three hundred kilometres away from the capital, and this makes the maritime traffic vitally important. Thus one of the prerogatives of insular life is the little port, with its own individual character, of each island. The coral reef is less broken than on Tahiti, and rich in *motu*, tiny islets surrounded with a corona of blond sand, that makes up an inseparable part of the islands' identity.

Travellers coming back from Raiatea, Huahine or Maupiti make the distinctions and differences very clear. If it is not in the relatively small number of beaches then it is in the villages, in authentic country roads, accommodation in private homes, in the animation of a quayside or the radiant solitude of a *motu* that visitors can experience pleasures and emotions of a higher order, thanks to the intimacy of an easy-going, natural way of life that is not just promised, but preserved, by the "Isles Beneath The Wind".

Fishing for the people of the Leeward Islands is governed by traditional relationships: Raiatea is the centre for bonito fishing; Huahine is famous for its fish enclosures. This image of a man mending his net serves as a reminder of the meaning of time taken through care and attention to detail in the maintenance of the worker's tools.

Huahine

Huahine has the peculiarity of consisting of two islands: Huahine Nui in the north, and Huahine Iti in the south, both washed by the same lagoon inside a single reef. They are joined by a bridge over a channel that can also be crossed on foot at low tide. Two extinct volcanoes, Turi and Puhuerei, dominate the site, like two tutelary deities. The broken shoreline is fringed with quiet white beaches that offer a full sense of the beauties of the lagoon.

Whether coming from the airport or from a sea landing across the Avamoa Pass, visitors converge on Fare, the most important community, where all the services and businesses relating to tourism and to island life have their headquarters. It is, in fact, a pleasant idyll, a well-shaded and lively village where arriving steamers loaded with merchandise, or those readying to carry off the local produce, throw everyone into a state of joyous bustle.

Beyond its natural charm, Huahine has a good deal of other interest. The island is especially rich in the archaeological vestiges that are to be found all over the Leewards. From the sites of Vaito'otia and Fa'ahia, researchers have discovered not only stone tools, but also remains of wooden objects datable to between 850 and 1100 B.C., the oldest so far found in Polynesia. The wonderfully diverse lagoon of Maeva shelters a stilt village of multicoloured bamboo. There, too, are the ruins of chiefly houses, their platforms jutting over the water, bearing witness to the far-off history of Huahine, as do the great Manunu *marae* and the others at the foot of the volcano Maua Tapu ("Sacred Mountain"). Where the lagoon of Maeva meets the sea, V-shaped traps await the fish when the tide goes out.

Nowadays, tourism makes up an important part of the economic life of Huahine, targeted at those who will fall in love with its ambience and its relaxed hospitality. There is also the quiet development of a special kind of agriculture, the growing of watermelons upon the *motu*, which has good flat surfaces improved by the digging of holes and filling them with imported topsoil. New crops are being added to the list: capsium, tomatoes and cucumbers show up alongside the melons regularly in the Papeete markets, giving the active little island something of a reputation.

A softened landscape and a road that brings together the fantasies of bays and peninsulas, Hauhine is a paradise for trampers, bicyclists and those who prefer to explore on horseback, which is luckily not difficult to arrange.

What is there to do on an island, after a day spent fishing or tilling the imported soil on the motu? Gossip, music, a game of bowls or billiards? This is a long way from the agitations and temptations of Papeete; distractions, conviviality itself, must virtually be invented.

Raiatea

Raiatea is the most important island in the Leeward archipelago. Sharing its lagoon with Tahaa, the two islands have an area of 282 km² between them, more than two thirds of the archipelago's total surface. Raiatea is also the tallest, with Mount Te Faroaiti rising to 1,033 m, and the liveliest as well: its capital Uturoa, the administrative headquarters of the whole group, is something more than just a village.

But prestige also comes to Raiatea from another source, and to an exceptionally high degree: the island's old name, Havai'i, ties it historically to the mythical origin of Polynesian gods and traditions, and the paradise of the old religion.

One need only follow the road back toward the village of Ogoa in the southeast of the island to find the vast ceremonial complex of Teputapuata and get an idea of the political-religious role that sacred Raiatea once played in Polynesian life. Teputapuata is an immense *marae*, the oldest of all the royal *marae* of Polynesia, and was built in the days of the is-

The boat is king at Raiatea: the bonito boats, 12-metre vessels with a team of two or three fishermen who can expect an annual yield of more than 20 tons, and the pleasure boats all over the lagoon between the twinned islands.

land's remotest history. It is known as the "international" *marae*, because it used to be the meeting place for religious functions gathering the people of the Society Islands with those of more distant archipelagos; this is where the cult of 'Oro began. Raiatea's royal family acquired its own prestige from the island's reputation, and exerted great influence on the political evolution of Eastern Polynesia, Tahiti in particular, through networks of kinship and marriage. This is the presumptive meaning of the myth that tells how Tahiti emerged from the water as a by-product of the splitting of another island into two: Raiatea and Tahaa.

The town of Uturoa brings us back to the present, with all the amenities of the modern world, including a secondary school, a hospital, banks, hotels and some thirty commercial establishments. A dynamic market and numerous shops make the town the second-ranked settlement after Papeete. New economic orientations are now in the developing stage: Raiatea is following Tahiti in taking on the part of a support centre for bonito fishing, while Tahaa has

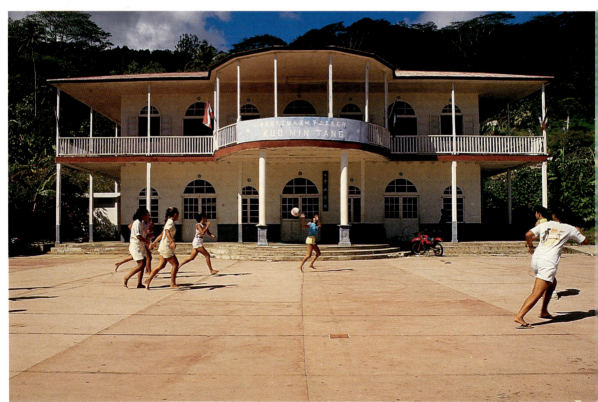

turned to aqua-culture, raising the value of its side of the lagoon through mussel farming.

In Raiatea, the raising of cattle and poultry has to some extent replaced certain traditional activities. If this has lost the island some of the affection of the kind of tourist that wants to find nothing but idyllic beaches in Polynesia, it provides the Territory with an authentic "province", for those who know how to see it, less tied down to the economics of tourism, bent on making good use of its resources.

Tahaa

Raiatea's little sister island across their common lagoon, a chunk of greenery flanked by paradisiacal islets, Tahaa, has no passable coastal roads. The little cemetery of the village of Vaitoare holds the remains of Rarahu, the original of the Tahitian child-woman in Pierre Loti's *Marriage*. Another village, Patio, is famous for the quality of its sailing-pirogue teams.

The noble past of Raiatea: the Taputapuatea marae side by side with contemporary life, where youth takes an increasingly important place (opposite page). Below: in spite of the growing number of salaried workers, traditional agriculture still persists, and it is always possible to visit the vanilla auction at Tahaa or the copra-drying on Raiatea.

Bora Bora

Bora Bora is a magical name that calls forth the mental picture of the perfect South Seas paradise. The crenellated mountain rising from a lagoon in which every nuance of blue and green is at play, the coral crown embellished with *motu*, make up one of the loveliest landscapes in the world. Small in size (38 km²), the island is dominated by the twin peaks of Otemanu (727 m) and Pahia (619 m).

Like the other Leeward Islands, Bora Bora, known in the old times as Vavau, has a long history. Its powerful chiefs exercised an important political influence as the reputation of its valiant warriors spread through the archipelago. The art of its pirogue-makers was famous — but has now fallen into neglect. That distant history left its mark in numerous *marae*, mostly, like the celebrated Vaiotaha, vanished, but some fortunately restored. The old fortifications had almost disappeared by the time in the modern era when Bora Bora, alone among the islands of French Polynesia, was invaded — a double invasion, and a friendly one, to be exact, since the military base that the Americans built in 1942 was never threatened; the Japanese eastward drive was halted the same year. Nevertheless, there were 4,500 men whose presence must have had some effect on insular habits. In four months, the Americans built a 2,000-metre airstrip on Motu Mute, which is still in use. Thus, until the inauguration of the international airport of Tahiti-Faaa, Bora Bora was the only island that could accommodate the big airliners.

This was the background for the second invasion, that of the astonished tourists. White sand beaches, azure lagoons and a profusion of flowers are the treasures to be shared with those who come here to discover the colours of their dreams in the waking world. Each year brings 20,000 of them, to an island whose population is less than 3,500. As is to be expected, a good number of these inhabitants work in the restaurants and hotels whose bungalows stand in the water along the perimetre of Vaitape, the island's administrative centre. Others devote themselves to the production of souvenirs, from curios to shell-necklaces. Such is the touristic vocation of Bora Bora. But when a place and people can give so many a moment of true happiness, is it not reason enough for pride?

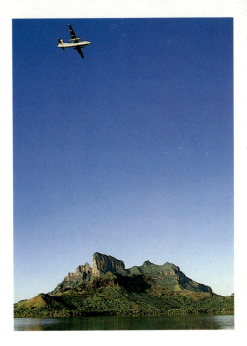

Several daily flights serve Bora Bora from Papeete. The predilection of tourists for this island has not spoiled its traditional qualities; the dancers continue to raise applause and the fishermen are known as some of the most skillful in the archipelago. And the many motu *of the lagoon, between sea and sky, are an ineffable satisfaction to the eye.*

Maupiti

Maupiti, a tiny closed universe, perfectly formed, protected, identity preserved. Seabirds circle a basalt peak reaching 380 m. Below, a riot of trees and flowers hides the *fare* of fishermen. Ruined *marae*, including that at Vaiahu, lurk over the lagoon, the only approach to which requires a fairly serious navigator at the tiller.

But boats are the only transport to the village of Vaien, by the quiet internal sea; the airport is on the *motu* whose broad crescent prefigures the shape of an atoll. Here, sixteen graves dating from the ninth century, the earliest period of the Society Islands' history, were discovered.

Even here, on the relatively isolated *motu*, changes may be seen. On its most extended parts, inhabitants now find land enough to cultivate various kinds of melon to supplement the fish which forms the bulk of their diet and income.

On Maupiti, people are involved in both fishing and agriculture, and indeed they travel by boat to their fields, on the motu *surrounding the island. The trip back offers the chance to bring a load of coconuts and a provision of giant clams, of which the reef has plenty.*

The Tuamotu Archipelago

According to Tahitian mythology, the god Tukerai, a sort of cross between Neptune and Hercules, decided one day to try shaking the sea. A terrific storm followed, and underwater currents hove a 1,500 km line of sand and rock out of the sea bottom: the Tuamotu archipelago. Magellan's fleet, in an *enfilade* row, sailed right through them, miraculously without seeing a single one. The Portuguese Queiros "discovered" them in 1605, and Bougainville dubbed them the "Dangerous Islands".

The Dangerous Archipelago

This designation is well deserved: countless ships, indeed, have crashed into reefs here rising from nowhere under their bows; countless ships punctured or torn on the sharp points of the coral. Even the present writer has experienced the reef's combined violence of the sea and wind on board an apparently solid boat which was annihilated in less than two hours; by dawn the next day a fine teak sailboat had been reduced to a few planks drifting around an atoll. It is a rare year when no schooner from the inter-island traffic "climbs up the reef", as the locals say, and smashes itself there. And today we have nautical instructions, detailed maps, perfected navigation instruments, while the sailors of the old times had nothing but their compasses and their instinct. It is because these coral rings scarcely rise more than two or three meters above the water surface. At night in heavy seas, it is impossible to see them coming, and the currents are on the violent side.

Today the isolation of Tuamotu has been partly broken by regular inter-island ferry services, and the Paumotu people, veteran navigators, can use outboard-motor canoes to communicate from one atoll to another in a few hours, a journey that could have taken a few days not so long ago. Radio, video, and solar energy all speed up development, to which the airplane makes an important contribution. Some thirty airfields accommodate safe evacuations, rapid-deployment expeditions for fresh fish, and tourism based in Rangiroa and Manihi offering a few people the revelation of a universe of ineffable beauty.

On the atolls, the brightly-coloured churches (left) — also sometimes in dazzling white — are a symbol of village unity. The birds are divided into the migratories, including frigatebirds, petrels and terns, and the sedentaries: doves, warblers, and the very rare and endangered Tahitian lorikeet (above).

The Atolls

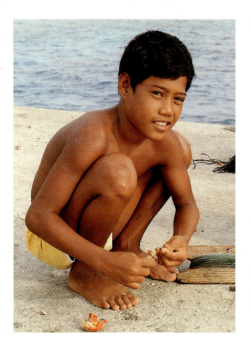

Of the 77 islands of the Tuamotu, 76 are atolls, narrow rings of sand and coral topped by coconut palms, circling emerald lagoons teeming with fish, crustaceans, molluscs, strange madrepore corals, and the passing shadows of sharks. The poor soil is hardly cultivable; the inhabitants live on copra and fishing.

Nor is there fresh water, only a few brackish wells and cisterns for collecting rainwater. Some atolls have no way out to the sea; others have one or several passes through which ships can come for the Edenic haven of the lagoon. There are no more than 6,000 people living in the entire archipelago. Many atolls remain uninhabited outside the seasons of fishing and copra harvest. Brutally put to the test by the cyclones of 1983, the atolls are now starting to re-cover their vitality. As in many of the islands of French Polynesia, the introduction and use of solar energy tend to improve daily life in this world of silent beauty.

The only sounds are the thunder of the waves breaking on the reef, the dull crash of a coconut, and the cries of the sea-birds.

The 77th island of the Tuamotu archipelago is Makatea, a 28 km² chunk of minerals 60 m thick, floating on the ocean. Its whitish cliffs and the holes on the surface, giving it the look of an enormous Gruyere, cover rich phosphate deposits. Unexploited since 1966, the island has been given back to the birds that built it.

Periculture

Over recent years, the Tuamotu islands and people have seen a trend to raising the pearl oyster *Pinctada margaritifera*. This mollusc can yield, after a delicate grafting operation, a black pearl, or to be exact a dark grey or grey-green *poe rava* pearl, coveted by pearl-lovers everywhere. There are currently 60 cooperatives and some 20 farms representing this promising industry.

In the Tuamotu archipelago, 50 percent of the population is under 15 years old. There are schools on almost every island to encourage people to stay. Below: fishing is still the main activity, and Tuamotu provides 70 percent of the fish sold on the Tahiti market.

The Marquesas

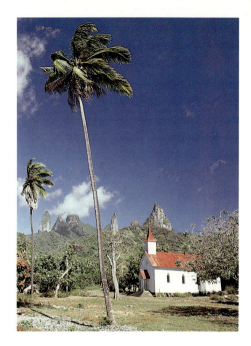

This is a group of a dozen islands stretching over 350 kilometres from north to south, of which only half are inhabited. No lagoons, only sheer cliffs. Deep valleys between keen notched mountains reaching 1,200 m at Hiva Oa and Nuku Hiva, and about 1,000 m on Fatu Hiva and Tahuata. These are the "Islas Marquesas de Mendoza", so named by Alvaro de Mendaña, the first European to pass, in 1595.

But in the third century of the current era, it is believed, the Polynesians themselves passed through the Marquesas near the end of their long eastward migration. From this base, they might have pushed out to Easter Island and Hawaii, and colonized Tahiti and the Society Islands. Thus they became the first true discoverers of these islands, and of French Polynesia.

Finely sculpted wooden objects, ornamented pounding-stones, rock-carvings, striking *tiki* made of tuff or basalt, and the immense platforms of small stones called *paepae*, are the remarkable remnants of the Marquesan culture, incontestably the richest and most original in the Polynesian triangle.

The six inhabited islands add up about 6,500 people. The northwest group includes Ua Uka, Ua Pou and Nuku Hiva, each with its own airport; Taiohae, in Niku Hiva, is the administrative and economic centre of the archipelago. Nuku Hiva is also the home of the valley of Taipivai where Herman Melville sought refuge in 1841 after jumping ship from a whaler, the episode eventually providing the germ for *Typee*. The islands of the southeast, Fatu Huku, Motane and Fatu Hiva, surround the twins Hiva Oa and Tahuata. Atuona, the principal village of Nuku Hiva, is the centre of activity at this end.

The incomparable Bay of the Virgins on Fatu Hiva, the wild horses of the plateaus, the statues on Nuku Hiva are just a few of the natural and archaeological sites that make the Marquesas fascinating. The population, which came close to extinction at the beginning of this century, deserves more than a brief mention. Today it is florishing again, the communes are dynamic and a sustained effort to develop the archipelago's own resources gives Marquesans a new perspective worthy of an out-of-the-ordinary personality.

Above: a church on Ua Pou island, whose jagged peaks are typical. Opposite: Max Radiguet wrote that the valleys of the Marquesas, seen from the heights, are like vast baskets of greenery with mirrors at the bottom.

101

On September 10, 1901, Paul Gauguin left Tahiti on the Croix du Sud. *He landed on the 16th at Nuku Hiva and moved into the village of Atuona, where he had his "House of Delight" built. Sick and subject to inextricable worries, he still produced some of his best work (*And the Gold of Their Bodies, 1902*), painting up till the day of his death, May 8, 1903. Not far from his tomb in Atuona are the remains of another fugitive who came to the Marquesas to seek peace and a different way of life: the poet and singer Jacques Brel, who arrived in 1975 and died three years later. The Bay of Hane (opposite) at Ua Uka illustrates the melancholy character of the Marquesan shores.*

The Gambier Archipelago

The impression of mystery is explicable to those who realize that the peopling of the archipelago is itself something of a mystery. It is believed that Mangareva was a stop on the Polynesian migration from the Marquesas toward Pitcairn and Easter Islands. The original Mangarevans may have come from the Cook Islands, considering the islands' pattern of colonisation as it is now understood. It is a relatively recent past, around the 13th century, evidenced by a number of *marae*, some of which were subsequently covered up by another form of civilisation: in fact this was the site of the first Catholic mission in Polynesia, established when Fathers Carré and Laval and Brother Murphy disembarked at Mangareva, on their way from Valparaiso August 7, 1834.

Southeast of the Tuamotu Islands is an immense round lagoon containing eight high islands constituting the Gambier Archipelago. Their "mainland" of 1,500 hectares is Mangareva, whose principal village of Rikitea is the capital. At 1,600 km from Tahiti, the Gambiers are at one extremity of French Polynesia, in an isolation that regular air and sea communications have only recently been able to break. Mangareva, whose modest (441 m) outline is often blurred by mist or a brief storm, has the look of a place with a perplexing past and a strange destiny.

With their evangelical passion came a fever for monument-building, erecting more than a hundred structures on the main island alone, including weavingworks, workshops, convent, seminary, chapels, churches, down to the cathedral of Rikitea, dating from 1841, which counted 2,000 worshippers, about the same figure as the population of the time. Most of the buildings are in ruins, and their architecture, more European than tropical, can leap from a Périgord-Byzantine pigeon-coop to an altogether Romanesque abbey, both situated near the monumental porch where the stupefied traveller first disembarks.

Now less isolated, the Gambiers and their 547 inhabitants live on fishing and kitchen gardening, profiting also from the revival of periculture and mother-of-pearl carving. The silent beauty of the great lagoon and the odd images of the past create a melancholy that is just as bewitching as the brilliance of the happiest Polynesian islands.

The Gambiers are a different time-world, in the bizarre atmosphere of ruins and monuments from an unparalleled human adventure, in the shade of a cathedral where solemn processions still file by.

The Austral Archipelago

This is the southernmost, and hence the coldest, archipelago of French Polynesia. It is formed by five fairly high islands (437 m at Raivavae), of which Tubuai, the largest, is the capital, with a 23 km road around its coast, bordered with *aito* or iron trees. Its isolation is reflected by its slower, less bustling pace: few automobiles here, where the scooter is king, and horses continue to be popular on this exquisite island of hills through which one may wander freely and where, at the end of the day, a cool breeze, a bit of hedgerow, a potato field, a meadow of grazing bovines create unexpected vistas, bringing on feelings one does not expect in a Polynesian archipelago. Rugged houses, white with coral lime, remind you that even in July and August you might feel the need for a light sweater. On the shore one can see the fortifications where the *Bounty* mutineers anchored before fleeing to Pitcairn. At Rurutu, horseback trails crisscross the hills like spiderwebs, suggesting the prospect of a good day's preoccupation for the tourist. The village of Avera is typical of this exceptional archipelago, with its taro plantations and its boxy white houses.

Rimatara, a low-lying verdant island, lacks an adequte harbour for boats, but has fine white beaches for any interested tourist. It is a historical oddity as well, having formed a separate kingdom, together with Rurutu, that joined France only in 1935. As for Raivavae, which is said to be homeland of the loveliest women of Polynesia, it is a cheerful island, surrounded by a luminous lagoon, with monumental stone statues evoking a romantic past.

Charming panadanus hats, soft *peue*, brilliant scarlet *tifaifai* with hand-sewn decorative motives, make up the craft specializations of the Australs, presenting a veritable symphony of colour and texture. But, although they are not yet the "breadbasket" of Tahiti, livestock and vegetable raising are taking on more importance year by year, establishing a non-tourist-based economy.

Last, the furthest south and the most elevated (650 m), the island where there are more women than men, is Rapa. With no coconut trees but a rich soil watered by storms, its taro culture and other vegetable gardening, Rapa stands isolated, the border sentry against the austral infinities.

Rapa, French Polynesia's "cold" island, offers a striking contrast with its rustic-charmed, gentle-terrained sisters. Ancient fortifications, typical of the Maori pa, *dominate the slopes of the old volcanic crater that shapes the island round the bay of Ahurei. Terraces built into the steep flanks of the rock, walls of dry stones, observation posts and entrenchments made up a system of defense protecting a reservoir of drinking water.*

At a latitude of 27° south, Rapa faces the full force of the winds of the open sea, giving it a certain roughness of temperment. All the more reason for trying to supply a bit of charm to the facts of everyday life, as in the Sunday services, when the inhabitants of the island's only village, Haueri, get together and decorate their hats with flowers and the famous and well-beloved plaits of pandanus leaf.

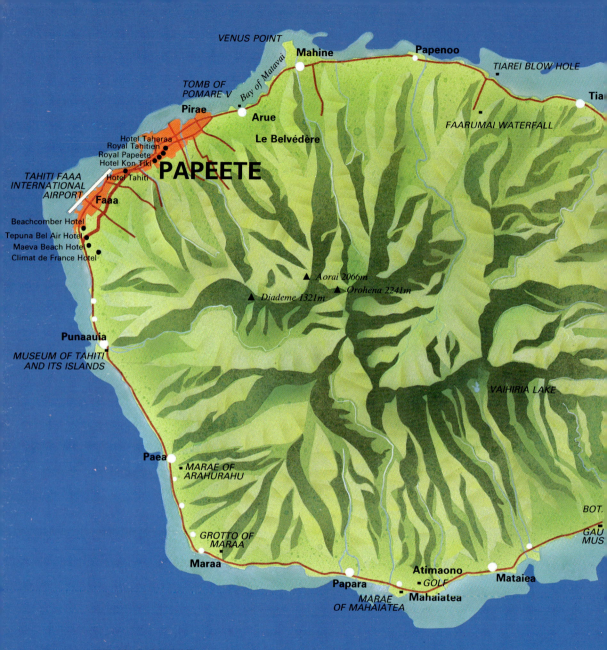

VENUS POINT

Mahine

Papenoo

TIAREI BLOW HOLE

TOMB OF
POMARE V

Bay of Matavai

Tia

Pirae

Arue

FAARUMAI WATERFALL

Hotel Taheraa
Royal Tahitien
Royal Papeete
Hotel Kon Tiki
Hotel Tahiti

Le Belvédère

PAPEETE

TAHITI FAAA
INTERNATIONAL
AIRPORT

Faaa

Beachcomber Hotel
Tepuna Bel Air Hotel
Maeva Beach Hotel
Climat de France Hotel

▲ *Aorai 2066m*

▲ *Orohena 2241m*

▲ *Diademe 1321m*

Punaauia

*MUSEUM OF TAHITI
AND ITS ISLANDS*

VAIHIRIA LAKE

Paea

*MARAE OF
ARAHURAHU*

BOT.

*GROTTO OF
MARAA*

GAU
MUS

Maraa

Atimaono
· *GOLF*

Mataiea

Papara

Mahaiatea

*MARAE
OF MAHAIATEA*

TAHITI

FRENCH POLYNESIA

MARQUESAS ARCHIPELAGO

Leeward Islands

TUAMOTU ARCHIPELAGO

SOCIETY ARCHIPELAGO

Windward Islands

TROPIC OF CAPRICORN

AUSTRAL   ARCHIPELAGO

GAMBIER ISLANDS

ena

BOUGAINVILLE'S ANCHORAGE

Hitiaa

Faaone

ravao

Afaahiti

Pueu   *COOK'S ANCHORAGE*   Tautira

eari

ARDEN TH

PENINSULA

OF

TAIARAPU

GROTTO OF MAUI

Vairao

▲ *Roniu 1332m*

ENGRAVED STONES

GROTTO OF ANAHIE

Practical Information

French Polynesia

French Polynesia consists of 4,000 km² of islands scattered over 4 million km² of ocean.

There are 117 islands divided into five archipelagoes: the Society Islands, which consist of the Windward Islands (Tahiti and Moorea) and Leeward Islands (Raiatea, Tahaa, Tetiatoa, Huahine, Bora Bora, Maupiti); the Tuamotu Archipelago; the Gambier Archipelago; the Marquesas Islands; and the Austral Archipelago. These islands are either high and volcanic or low and of coral origin.

Local Time
Local time is GMT-10. French Polynesia is two hours behind San Francisco, five hours behind New York and 11 hours behind Paris.

Climate
Tropical, hot and humid, cooled by the trade winds. There are two seasons: one mainly dry and cool, from March to November (70ºF to 80ºF); the other hot and humid, from November to March (80ºF to 95ºF).

Flora
Sub-tropical. Specially exuberant along the coast and in the valleys: coconut, mango, breadfruit, flamboyant, bougainvillea, frangipani, tiare and many others. On the mountainside the vegetation is poorer and more indigenous: casuarina, ferns, bamboo, Tahitian chestnut or *mape*, wild banana or *fei*, purau, pandanus.

Fauna
Rather poor. Only amongst the birds are there several interesting indigenous species: white-tailed tropicbird, reef heron, grey duck, crested or swift tern, the rare Tahitian lorikeet and the very common Indian mynah. Amongst the insects: cockroaches, ants, mud dauber, wasps, bees, spiders, flies and mosquitos. A large scolopendra, the centipede, has a very painful sting. There are no reptiles, except small lizards. On the other hand the sea fauna is very rich, both in the lagoon and in the open sea: more than 300 species of fish; shell-fish such as crabs, lobsters and shrimps; also oysters, mother-of-pearl, clams, etc. Tides are regular; low at 6am and pm; high at 12am and pm. These are solar tides and of limited movement.

History
The inhabitants of French Polynesia are descendants of Maoris who migrated there in the first century A.D. When the Europeans arrived in the 18th century, they found an organized and well-established society in Polynesia. Several expeditions were necessary to chart or explore all the islands. Tahiti was visited for the first time in 1767 by Wallis, then by Bougainville in 1768, Cook in 1769 and Bligh in 1788. The latter became famous because of the mutiny on the *Bounty*.

Cook also travelled to the Leeward Islands and certain islands of the Tuamotu archipelago. The Marquesas were discovered by the Spanish in 1595; then were visited by Cook in 1774 and by Ingraham in 1791. Th

Australs were gradually explored first by Cook in 1768, then by Gayangos, Varela and Vancouver. Until 1880 Tahiti was governed by the Pomare dynasty. It then became a French colony, including the neighbouring islands. In 1957 French Polynesia acquired the status of a French overseas territory.

Population
165,000 inhabitants in French Polynesia. 74% live on the Windward Islands and over 2/3 of these on Tahiti itself. Polynesian Maoris represent 75% of the population. Europeans represent 8.6%, Chinese 7%, half-Europeans 7.2%, half-Chinese 0.9% and others 1.3%.

Religion
Two religions represent the vast majority: Protestants 50% and Catholics 35%. Mormons, 7th Day Adventists and Jehovah's Witnesses 15%.

Language
French and Tahitian are the official languages. Puamotu, Marquesan and Cantonese are also spoken. English is spoken in hotels, restaurants, shops, etc.

Economy
Mainly based on fishing, agriculture and tourism. Since the establishment of the C.E.P. (Pacific Experimentation Centre) in 1960, due to the French nuclear tests, the Polynesian economy has undergone a great change. Through taxes, the C.E.P. has payed large sums of money on imported merchandise sent to Hao, Mururoa and Fangataufa. The C.E.P. and the C.E.A. have also given work to many. This economic boom has brought with it a frantic consumer society that has sent prices sky-rocketing. The artificial prosperity created by the C.E.P. is now ending. The problems incurred in finding an economic balance in order to avoid total dependence on the outside world have resulted in much hardship. A new economy based on tourism, agriculture and fishing is now being encouraged.

Administration and Political Organization
A new statute of partial self-rule came into effect on September 6, 1984 giving local government extended power. The French State is represented by a high commissioner appointed by the Government. He is in charge of foreign affairs, law, national defence, police and legal tender. Territorial authorities handle other competencies. The territory is represented in Paris by two deputies, one senator and one social and economic counselor. A territorial assembly of 30 members, elected every five years, is in charge of territorial legislation. The president is elected by the Assembly and appoints his ministers who are in charge of the Executive.

How to Get There
By plane: eight international airlines fly to French Polynesia: Air France, Intercontinental Airlines, U.T.A., Air New Zealand, Qantas, Lan Chile, Hawaiian Airlines, Minerve. The international airport is at Faaa, five kilometres from Papeete.

Entry Formalities — Immigration Officials
A passport and sometimes a visa is needed for all except French citizens, who only need their identity

card. An American visa is needed for those stopping over in the U.S.A. unless in transit. A return or continuation ticket is also required, or a deposit equivalent to the price of a return ticket. A dispensation of this requirement might be obtained.

Customs

Up to 200 cigarettes or 50 cigars and two litres alcoholic beverage may be brought in.

What to Wear

No formalities; light cotton clothes and swimsuits. Perhaps also a cardigan and a light raincoat. Everything can be bought in Papeete, but prices are rather high.

Exchange Rates

The monetary unit is the French Pacific franc (CPF). 1.00 FFR = 18.18 CFP, 100 CFP = 5.50 FFR. The exchange rate for foreign currencies will vary with the fluctuation of the French franc to which the Pacific franc is tied. US$ 1.00 = 15.95 FFR.

News Media

There is the government radio/television station RFO (Radio France Outre-Mer) with colour television broadcasts daily from 3:30 to 11pm to Tahiti, Moorea and the Leewards Islands, plus a few private radio stations, among others: RTA and FM 100.

Two daily newspapers in French, *La Dépêche* and *Les Nouvelles*; a magazine, *Tahitirama*, plus a complimentary English language weekly publication, *Tahiti Sun Press*. Also, a practical guide, *Le Trouvtou* (addresses, advice), for those who wish to know Tahiti better.

International newspapers and magazines arrive weekly by air mail.

Health

There is one hospital in Tahiti at Mamao; two clinics: Cardella and Pao Fai; and one medical institute: Malardé, for tropical disease research. There are also private doctors, dentists and chemists.

The other islands have at least a surgery, with a doctor and a nurse.

The most common hazards are dengue fever, fish poisoning, cutting oneself on the coral, stonefish stings.

Travelling

Land transportation consists of *le truck* — Tahitian bus, typical and inexpensive; taxis, with the price-list established by the government shown in each car; hire cars in Tahiti, Moorea, Bora Bora, Raiatea, Huahine.

Air Polynesia links the islands, and so do several ferries. From Tahiti there are the following flights: Moorea in 7 min (15 km); Huahine in 40 min (170 km); Raiatea in 45 min (220 km); Bora Bora in 50 min no stops and 1 hour 10 min stopping at Raiatea (260 km); from Bora Bora to: Maupiti in 20 min (315 km); Rangiroa in 1 hour (350 km); Manihi in 2 hours 40 min stopping at Rangiroa (520 km); Tubuai (Australs) in 1 hour 50 min (670 km); Ua Uka and Hiva Oa (Marquesas) in 7 hours 50 min stopping at Rangiroa and Manihi (1400 km). Air Polynesia, 42.39.39.

Air Tahiti flies to Moorea from Tahiti every 30 minutes. Baggage allowance is 10 kg.

Local Crafts

Interesting objects to buy: sculptures in wood (*tiki, umete*...), nacres, shells and shell jewelry, wicker-work (hats, baskets, mats...), *pareu* material, clothes made of hand-printed material, *tifaifai* (kind of patchwork: cushion-covers and bedspreads), *tapa* (painted bark), shells.

Tourist Information

The tourist bureau (Office du Tourisme, OPATTI) operates at Faaa Airport and on Boulevard Pomare, B.P. 65, Papeete, tel. 42.96.26; open throughout the week from 7:30am to 5pm, and on Saturdays from 9am to 4pm.

Helpful Hints

- The best time to visit Polynesia is from May to October.
- Tap water is fit for drinking.

- Alternating current (60 cyc.) is of 110 or 220 volts.
- Tipping is against the rules of hospitality.
- Shops are open from 7:30 to 11:30am and from 2 to 5pm.
- Prices are official: no bargaining.
- The central post office is in Papeete. There are post offices on almost all the other islands. Telephone links between Tahiti, Moorea, Raiatea, Huahine, Bora Bora are now automatic. Communication between the other islands is by radiotelephone. Tahiti is linked by satellite to the international telephone system and may now be dialed direct.

Tahiti

Tahiti lies in the South Pacific halfway between Australia and the U.S.A. It is the main island of French Polynesia, covering 1,042 km^2. Tahiti is a volcanic island, very fertile, formed by two volcanoes united by an isthmus. It is surrounded by coral reefs that protect the lagoons. The highest mountain is Mount Orohena, 2,234 m.

Population
123,000 people live in Tahiti, 78,000 of whom live in Papeete. The Tahitians are known for their extreme kindness, goodwill and natural gaiety.

Hotels
De luxe:
- *Beachcomber*, Faaa, B.P. 601	42.51.10
- *Hyatt Regency Taharaa*, Arue, B.P. 1015	48.11.22
- *Sofitel Maeva Beach*, Punaauia, B.P. 600	42.80.42

First Class:
- *Holiday Inn*, Vallée de Tipaerui, B.P. 32	42.67.67
- *Hôtel le Mandarine*, Papeete, B.P. 302	42.16.33
- *Hôtel Tahiti*, Papeete, B.P. 416	42.95.50
- *Ibis Papeete*, B.P. 4545	42.32.77
- *Ibis Punaauia*, B.P. 576	42.60.40
- *Pacific Papeete*, B.P. 111	42.95.99
- *Princesse Heiata*, Pirae, B.P. 5003	42.81.05
- *Royal Papeete*, Papeete, B.P. 919	42.01.29
- *Royal Tahitien*, Pirae, B.P. 5001	42.81.13
- *Te Puna Bel Air*, Faaa, B.P. 6634	42.82.24

Hotels on the circle island tour:
- *Le Petit Mousse*, Papara, B.P. 32	57.42.07
- *Station touristique de Puunui*, Vairao	57.19.20

A number of other possibilities exist regarding lodging: small hotels, private homes. The addresses for these establishments are available at the Tourist Information Office, at the airport or in town on Boulevard Pomare.

Restaurants
Hotel restaurants have not been included in the following list.

Papeete and surroundings:
French restaurants:
- *Acajou*, Boulevard Pomare, Fare Tony	42.87.58
- *Le Belvédère*, Fare Rau Ape Route, Pirae	42.73.44
- *Le Bistrot du Port*, Avenue Bruat	42.55.09
- *Le Bougainville*, behind the cathedral	42.70.15
- *Le Captain Cook*, Hôtel Taharaa	48.11.22
- *Changuy*, Rue des Remparts	42.87.76
- *La Corbeille d'Eau*, seafront	43.77.14
- *La Crémaillère*, Chemin de Patutoa	42.09.15
- *Le Gauguin*, Hôtel Maeva Beach	42.80.42
- *Le Grillardin*, Rue Gauguin	43.09.90
- *Le Lion d'Or*, Rue Afarerii	42.66.50
- *Le Malibu*, Rue E. Ahne	42.95.97
- *Le Manava*, Avenue Bruat	42.02.91
- *La Maribaude*, Pamatai	42.82.52
- *Moana Iti*, Boulevard Pomare	42.65.24
- *La Petit Auberge*, Pont de l'Est	42.86.13

- *Le Rétro*, Vaima Centre   42.40.00

Chinese restaurants:
- *Dahlia*, Arue, Route de Ceinture   42.59.87
- *Le Dragon d'Or*, Rue Colette   42.96.12
- *Le Jade Palace*, Vaima Centre   42.02.19
- *Liou Foung*, Avenue du Prince-Hinoï   42.09.82
- *Le Mandarin*, Rue des Ecoles   42.99.03
- *Pitate Mamao*, Avenue G. Clemenceau   42.86.94
- *La Soupe Chinoise*, Rue Gauguin   42.97.48
- *Te Hoa*, Pirae   42.06.91
- *Waikiki*, Rue A. Leboucher   42.95.27

Other restaurants:
- *Baie d'Along*, Vietnamese, Avenue du Prince-Hinoï
                                              42.05.35
- *La Pizzeria*, Italian, on the seafront   42.98.30
- *Lou Pescadou*, pizzeria, Rue Cardella   43.74.26

Restaurants on the circle island tour:
- *Acajou*, Punaauia   43.45.06
- *Auberge du Pacifique*, Punaauia   43.98.30
- *Bob Tardieu*, Faaone   57.14.14
- *Captain Bligh*, Lagoonarium, Punaauia   43.45.06
- *Chez Coco*, Punaauia   58.21.08
- *L'Escale*, Taravao   57.18.51
- *Faratea*, Faaone   57.10.01
- *Marina Taina*, Punaauia   42.76.69
- *Mon Faré*, Mahina   48.22.23
- *Nahiti Nui*, Mahina   43.15.49
- *Nuutere*, Papara   57.41.15
- *Le Pari*, Teahupoo   57.13.44
- *Le Petit Mousse*, Papara   57.42.09
- *Le Pirate, Chez Jérôme*, Punaauia   43.68.13
- *Restaurant du Musée Gauguin*, Papeari   57.13.80
- *Le Routi*, Faaone   57.14.44
- *Taiarapu*, Taravao   57.11.51
- *Te Moana*, Lagoonarium, Punaaiua   58.29.91
- *La Trattoria*, Punaauia
- *VahineMoena*, Papara   57.41.70
- *Vahoata*, Mataeia   57.42.44

Rent-a-Car

Rates are according to mileage or on a daily basis and vary depending on the type of car rented.
The main rent-a-car agencies are:
- *André*, near Hotel Kon Tiki   42.94.04
- *Avis*, Rue Charles-Vienot   42.96.49
- *Europcar*, Boulevard Pomare   42.46.16

- *Hertz*, Rue Cdt-Destremeau   42.04.71
- *Location Daniel*, Faaa   42.30.04
- *Pacificar*, Rue des Remparts   42.43.64
- *Point Orange*, Avenue du Prince-Hinoï   42.14.14
- *Polynesian Rental*, airport   43.07.70
- *Robert*, Boulevard Pomare   42.97.20
- *T.T.T.*, Tipaerui Valley   42.76.39
- *Tahiti Rent-a-Car*, Fare Ute   42.74.49

Rent-a-Boat
- *Haurepe Charter*   42.80.27
- *Jac Boat*   42.28.65
- *Marina Taina*   42.76.69
- *Mer et Loisirs*   43.97.99
- *Revata Cruise*   43.28.21
- *Tahiti Aquatique*   42.22.32
- *Tahiti Yachting*   42.78.03

Airplane and Helicopter
- *Pacific Hélicoptère*   43.16.80
- *T.C.A.*   43.84.25
- *Tahiti Hélicoptère*   43.34.26

Celebrations

New Year's Day – March 5: Arrival of the Gospel – Easter Friday to Monday – May 1st – Ascension Day – Whit Sunday – July 14 (French national holiday) – All Saints – Armistice Day – Christmas.

The most important celebration is the *Tiurai*, which lasts at least two weeks beginning the week of July 14, including dancing contests, canoe races, horse races, javelin-throwing contests, etc.

Other important celebrations: Chinese New Year, Night of the Guitar, Ball of Tahiti in Times Gone By, Night of the Vahine and Tiare Day.

Sports

- *Fitness Club*	43.42.22
- *Club Equestre*	42.70.41
- *Poney Club de Tahiti*	43.15.82
- *Club de tir aux Pigeons* (clay pigeon shooting), Hôtel Taharaa	48.11.22
- *Tennis Club*, Fautaua Stadium	42.00.59
- *L'Eperon*	42.79.87
- *Club de Golf*, Atimaono, Mataeia	57.42.41
- *Golf at Hotel Taharaa*	48.11.23
- *Club Alpin* of M. Jay, Arue	48.10.59
- *Aéroclub*, Faaa	42.80.61
- *Club Aéronautique de Tahiti*, Faaa	42.84.84
- *Parachute Club*, Faaa	42.80.61
- *Bridge Club of Tahiti*	42.47.54
- *Bowling*, Arue P.K. 5.6	42.93.26

Water sports are varied and facilities exist in hotels as well as in sport clubs.

- *Haura Club*, sport fishing	42.89.10
- *Tahiti Aquatic*, Hôtel Maeva Beach	42.81.54 (ex.0951)
- *Tahiti Yacht Club*, P.K.4, Arue	42.78.03

Scuba- and skin-diving, etc.:

- *Bathy's Club*	42.46.77
- *Corail Sub*	43.62.51
- *Force 6*, Hôtel Beachcomber	42.51.10
- *Piscine*, Tipaerui	42.89.24
- *Ski nautique club*, Bel-Air	42.10.38
- *Tahiti Jet Ski Club*	57.42.85
- *Taravana Club*	57.23.99
- *Y.C.T./Centre de plongée*	42.23.55

Clubs

- *Lion's Club*, c/o Holiday Inn	42.67.67
- *Rotary Club*, Hôtel Maeva Beach	42.80.42

Nightlife

Local groups provide music in hotel discotheques. Most hotels put on shows with traditional Tahitian dancing.

A selection of bars and nightclubs in Papeete:

- *Le Bougainville*, Rue M. Tepano	43.15.36
- *Le Bounty Club*, discotheque, Rue des Ecole	42.93.00
- *La Cave*, Hôtel Royal Papeete	42.01.29
- *Le Chaplin's*, Boulevard Pomare	42.73.05
- *Le Club 5*, Rue des Ecoles	
- *Club 106*, Uranie quay	42.72.92
- *Club Rétro*, Vaime Centre	42.86.83
- *La Jonque*, at the port	42.73.05
- *Mayana Club*, Bruat Centre	43.82.29
- *Le Paradise*, seafront	42.73.05
- *Le Piano Bar*, Rue des Ecoles	42.88.24
- *Le Pirate*, Avenue Bruat	42.83.04
- *Le Star Circus*, Rue T. Jaussen	42.62.41
- *Le Tiki Room*, Hôtel Matavai	42.67.67
- *La Too Much*, Vaima Centre	42.81.05
- *Le Zizou Bar*, Boulevard Pomare	42.07.55

Some of the main cinemas:

- *Le Concorde 1 and 2*, Vaima Centre.
- *Hollywood 1 and 2*, Fare Tony.
- *Le Liberty*, Rue du Maréchal-Foch.
- *Mamao Palace*, Mamao.

There is also a Cultural Center at Pao Fai, which has a cine-club, theatre, library and dance school.

Museums

- *Gauguin Museum*, open every day, 9am to 5pm	57.10.58
- *Museum of Tahiti and its Islands*, Pointe des Pêcheurs, Punaauia, open Tuesday through Sunday, 8am to 5pm	58.34.76
- *Museum of the Discovery*, Pointe Venus, open every day, 9 to 12am	58.12.20
- *Museum of Shells*, Papara, open every day except Monday 9am to 5pm	
- *Pearl Museum*, Boulevard Pomare, Pao Fai	43.85.58

- *Papeari Botanical Gardens*, pk 51   57.11.07

Art Galleries
- *Galerie Jacques Laurent*, Vaima Centre   42.04.32
- *Galarie Noa Noa*, Boulevard Pomare   42.73.47
- *Galerie Oviri*, Punaauia   42.63.82
- *Galerie Vaimantic*, Vaima Centre   43.68.96
- *Tahiti Art* , seafront   42.97.43
- *Winkler Laurent* , Rue Jeanne d'Arc   42.92.52

Handicraft Centres
- *Centre des métiers d'arts*, Papeete   43.70.51
- *Pu Maohi*, Avenue du Régent Paraita   43.70.26
- *Pu Maohi Faati*, Avenue G. Clémenceau   42.63.65
- *Pu Tamatea*, Avenue Pomare V   43.97.62
- *Tahiti Perles Center*, Boulevard Pomare   43.85.58

Tours and Excursions
travel agencies and tour operators:
- *Aute Voyages*, B.P. 341 Papeete   42.66.07
- *C.G.M.*, B.P. 96   42.08.90
- *Club Med*   42.96.99
- *Manureva Tours*, B.P. 1745, Papeete   42.72.58
- *Pacific Travel*, B.P. 605, Papeete   42.93.85
- *Pacific Tours*, B.P. 2430   42.49.36
- *Tahiti Nui*, B.P. 718, Papeete   42.04.91
- *Tahiti Poroi*, B.P. 83, Papeete   42.00.70
- *Tahiti Tours*, B.P. 627, Papeete   42.78.70
- *Tahiti Voyages*, B.P. 485, Papeete   42.57.63
- *Teremoana Tours*, B.P. 475, Papeete   42.69.92
- *Vahine Tahiti Travel*, B.P. 1699, Papeete   42.44.83

- *Voyagence Tahiti*, B.P. 274, Papeete   42.72.13

Circle Island Tour

Going east: Papeete-Taravao:
- 2.5 km: Bain Loti — Fautaua River.
- 4.7 km: Arue, Tomb of King Pomare V.
- 5.4 km: Aure, James Normann Hall's house.
- 8.1 km: Arue, Taharaa coast and hotel.
- 11 km: Mahina, Point Venus, Matavai Bay.
- 11.7 km: Mahina, two roads into the mountains to the right, offering a splendid view of the sea.
- 13.2 km: Orofara leper village.
- 17.1 km: Papenoo Valley.
- 22 km: Tiarei, blow-hole.
- 22.5 km: Faarumai valley waterfalls
- 37.6 km: Hitiaa, Bougainville's anchorage.
- 39 km: Hitiaa, splendid view of the peninsula.
- 41.8 km: Hitiaa, Faatautia waterfalls.
- 53 km: Taravao village.

The peninsula via the east coast:
- 0.6 km: Afaahiti, mountain road towards a splendid view of Tahiti.
- 16.5-18 km: village, bay and river of Tautira, the "garden of Eden" where Robert Louis Stevenson lived.

Return to Taravao:
- 7.3 km: Toahotu, Zane Grey's territory.
- 8.5 km: Vairao, natural harbor; legendary hero Maui is said to have left his footprints on the reef.
- 18 km: village of Teahupoo; return to Taravao.

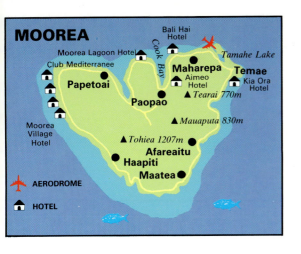

Going west: Taravao-Papeete

- 55 km: Papeari.
- 51.6 km: Papeari, Harrison W. Smith's Botanical Gardens and the Gauguin Museum.
- 50 km: Papeari, Gauguin Museum's restaurant.
- 48 km: Mataiea, road to Lake Vaihiria.
- 46.5 km: Mataiea, where Gauguin lived 1891-93.
- 44 km: Mataiea, Rupert Brooke's haven.
- 41 km: Papara, Atimaono golf course.
- 39.2 km: Papara, ruins of the great Mahaitea *marae*.
- 28.5 km: Paea, Paroa cave at Maraa.
- 22.5 km: Paea, *marae* in the Arahurahu valley.
- 14.6 km: Museum of Tahiti and its Islands.
- 12.6 km: Punaauia, a school indicated by the sign "2+2=4"; near the site where Gauguin once lived.
- 5.5 km: Faaa, international airport.
- Papeete.

Moorea

Moorea is some 17 km to the northwest of Tahiti.

Population

8,000 inhabitants throughout the five principal areas: Teavaro, Papetoai, Pao Pao, Afareaitu and Haapiti.

Access

By plane: the flight takes 10 minutes. Air Moorea and Air Tahiti have flights every 30 minutes.

By sea: leaving from Papeete-Moorea quay every day between 9 and 9:30 am. The trip takes slightly over one hour. The ferries are the following:

- *Keke III*	42.80.60
- *Moorea Ferry*	43.73.64
- *Tamarii Moorea VIII* and *2B*	56.13.92 or 42.76.50

Accomodation

Hotels:

- *Bali Hai Moorea*, B.P. 26, Moorea	56.13.52
- *Climat de Moorea*, B.P. 1017, Papetoai	56.15.48
- *Club Bali Hai*, B.P. 26, Moorea	56.13.68
- *Club Med Moorea*, B.P. 575, Moorea	42.96.99
- *Hotel Baie de Cook*, Pao Pao	
- *Hotel Captain Cook*, B.P. 1006, Moorea	56.21.00
- *Hotel Hibiscus*, B.P. 1009, Papetoai	56.12.20
- *Hotel Kaveka*, B.P.13, Moorea	56.18.30
- *Ibis Moorea*, B.P. 30, Moorea	56.10.50
- *Moorea Village*, B.P.1008, Moorea	56.10.02
- *Résidence Les Tipaniers*, B.P. 1002, Moorea	56.12.67
- *Sofitel Kia Ora*, B.P. 706, Moorea	56.12.90
- *Sofitel Tiare Moorea*, B.P. 205, Moorea	56.15.35
- *Te Puna Moorea Lagoon*, B.P. 11, Moorea	56.14.68

Other places to stay while in Moorea:

- *Chez Billy Ruta*	56.12.54
- *Coconut House*	56.18.98
- *Hotel Chez Pauline*, a small traditional inn with five rooms	56.11.26
- *Motel Albert Haring*	56.12.76

- *Residence Tiahura*   56.15.45

Other houses are also available for lodging. Their addresses are available at the Office of Tourism.

Restaurants

- *Chez Michel and Jackie*, Maharepa   56.11.08
- *Coconut House*, Maharepa   56.15.44
- *Coco's Restaurant*, B.P. 1023, Papetoai 56.10.63
- *L'Escargot Hotel Hibiscus*, Pk 27   56.12.20
- *Les Tipaniers*, Haapiti   56.12.67
- *Linareva*, Haapiti   56.15.35
- *L'Oasis*, Haapiti   56.18.94
- *Manava Nui*, Cook's Bay   56.22.00
- *New Hakka*, B.P. 341, Cook's Bay   56.12.19

Transportation

Taxi or bus: from hotels to airport and vice-versa.
Truck: upon arrival of ferries and other ships.
Rent-a-car:
- *Arii Rent-a-Car*, airport   56.11.03
- *Hertz*, airport   56.11.03
- *Pierre*, airport   56.12.48
- *Ruta Billy*, Haapiti   56.16.98

It is also possible to rent bicycles, mopeds or scooters, by the day or half-day.

Art Galleries

- *Galerie Api, Patrice Bredel*, Haapiti   56.13.57
- *Galerie Van der Heyde*, Cook's Bay   56.31.62

Excursions

The island tour is possible by car, as there are 60 km of good roads. What must be seen:
- Cook's Bay.
- Opunohu Bay.
- Vaiare Bay and Pierced Mountain.
- Churches and temples, namely: the octagonal temple of Papetoai; the Catholic mission of Haapiti with its two square towers; and the Catholic mission of Pao Pao with a nativity by Heyman.
- The *marae*: at Nuurua, at Maatea, Afareaitu and Titioro near the school of agriculture.
- The crater road, starting from the village of Pao Pao, crosses the pineapple plantations and arrives at a point from which a splendid view of both the Bay of Cook and of Opunohu can be observed, separated by Mount Rotui. The road descends towards Opunohu Bay crossing the agricultural college.
The hotels also organize picnics and excursions.

Raiatea

The second largest island in the Society Archipelago, a triangle-shaped 238 km^2. Raiatea is encircled by the same lagoon as Tahaa, the neighbouring island. The highest mountain is Te Faroaiti, at 1,033 m.

Population

The largest population in the Leeward Islands: 7,500 inhabitants of which 2,800 live in Uturoa, a small "capital" with a port, airport, school, hospital, government offices and several shops.

Access

By plane: Air Polynesia flies several times a day between Raiatea and Papeete. The direct flight is 45 minutes; stopping at Huahine, 65 minutes.

By ship: three ferries provide transportation between Papeete and Raiatea: *Raromatai Ferry* (43.90.42) on Tuesday and Friday; *Taporo IV* (42.63.93) on Monday, Wednesday and Friday; and the *Temehani* (42.98.83) Monday and Wednesday evenings.

Transportation

Truck: twice a day from Uturoa to the other villages and back (Opoa, Avera, Tevaitoa, Fetuna and Vaiaau). Also from the airport to Uturoa and Bali Hai Hotel.
Taxi: airport, Uturoa and Bali Hai Hotel.
Rent-a-car:
- *Mr. Guirouard, Motu Tapu Garage*, Uturoa 66.33.09
- *Raiatea Location*   66.34.06

Accommodation
- *Bali Hai Raiatea*, B.P. 252, Uturoa   66.31.49
- *Le Motu*, Uturoa   66.34.06

Restaurants
- *Bali Hai*, in the hotel   66.31.49
- *Jade Garden*, Uturoa   66.34.40
- *Le Motu*, Uturoa   66.34.06
- *Le Quay des Pecheurs*, Uturoa   66.36.83

Excursions
The circle island tour can be made by car, except for the southern coast. The principal sights: a visit to a *fare* at which an *umuti* or "fire dance" is done by villagers from Apooiti, opposite the Bali Hai Hotel in Tupua Bay; a visit to the most famous *marae* in Polynesia, the Taputapuatea *marae* (meaning "extended and very sacred"), a highlight of ancient Maori civilisation; *marae* of Tainuu at Tevaitoa, on the west coast; also *marae* ruins on Mount Toomaru (1,017 m).

Bali Hai Hotel organizes excursions by mini-bus and on the lagoon by speed-boat. It offers various sports: water-skiing, under-water diving and fishing, horse-riding, tennis and sailing at the *Uturoa Yacht Club*.

Tahaa

Tahaa faces Raiatea in the same lagoon. A circular island covering 82 km², its highest peaks are Mount Ohiri (590 m) and Mount Purauti (550 m). The southern coast has several deep bays.

Population
With a total population of 3,750 inhabitants, Tahaa is divided into eight districts: Hipu, Nuia, Tapuamu, Iripau, Ruutia, Vaitoare, Haamene and Faaha. The main village is Patio, which is the furthest from Raiatea.

Access
Only by boat. A ship departs from Uturoa every Wednesday and Friday at 12:30pm, arriving at Vaitoare and returning to Uturoa on the same day at 3pm.

Accommodation
Hotels:
- *Marina Iti*, B.P. 888, Uturoa   65.61.01
- *Tahaa Lagoon/Hibiscus*, B.P. 184, Haamene 65.61.06
- *Chez Diego et Françoise*   65.64.80

Pensions:
- *Chez Pascal*   65.60.42
- *Chez Siméon Chu*   65.53.00
- *Le Moana*   65.61.06

Excursions
In Vaitoare is the tomb of Rarahu, the Tahitian girl described in *The Marriage of Loti* (1882) by the French writer Pierre Loti. To visit the island, a road leads from Hipu to Tiuva and as far as Hurepiti Bay. To continue one must follow a small path. The mountain's rocks have different names according to the animals or things they resemble. The island tour can be made by boat, visiting the beautiful bays of Hurepiti, Apu, Haamene and Faaaha.

To rent a boat, go to the *Marina Iti*.

Tetiaroa

Tetiaroa, an atoll 47 km north of Tahiti, is formed by several coral islets surrounded by a reef. A small pass on the northwest border can be used by small boats. The island used to belong to the royal Pomare family and today is the property of actor Marlon Brando who has set up a tourist center: *Tetiaroa Village*.

Access

By plane: there are three flights a week between Tahiti and Tetiaroa, Wednesdays, Saturdays and Sundays. The flight lasts 20 minutes.

By boat: certain ferries stop at times to unload cargo and passengers.

Accommodation

Tetiaroa Village is a vacation village built in the Polynesian style. For reservations, write to *Tetiaroa Village*, B.P. 2418, Papeete. Cable address: Tetiaroa Papeete, tel. 58.13.02.

Huahine

Huahine lies 130 km to the northwest of Papeete and 32 km to the east of Raiatea. It is formed by two islands: Huahine Nui (large Huahine) whose highest peak is Mount Turi (669 m) and Huahine Iti (small Huahine) whose highest peak is Mount Puhuerei (462 m). The entire surface is 74 km².

Population

There are 4,000 inhabitants in Huahine. The island is divided into eight sections, four in Huahine Nui (Fare, the capital, with post office, police station and surgery; Fitii, Faie and Maeva) and four in Huahine Iti (Haapu, Parea, Tefarerii, Maroe).

Access

By plane: there are 14 flights a week from Tahiti by Air Polynesia. The flight takes 35 minutes.

By boat: three ferries depart from Papeete to Huahine: *Temehani II* Monday and Thursday at 5pm; *Taporo IV* Monday and Wednesday at 6pm; and *Raromatai Ferry*, Tuesday and Friday at 8:30pm.

Transportation

There is a road from Maeva to Parea, passing by Fare, Fitii and Haapu.

Both taxis and trucks are available at Fare, Parea and the airport.

The island tour can be made by taxi or mini-bus.

rent-a-car:
- *Avis Rent-a-Car*, Bali Hai Hotel   68.82.34
- *Francois Rent-a-Car*, address: François Lefoc, Village of Fare Huahine   68.82.76

Accommodation

- *Bali Hai Huahine*, Fare, B.P. 2   68.82.77
- *Hotel Bellevue*, Maroe, B.P. 21   68.82.76
- *Hotel Huahine*, Fare   68.82.69
- *Huahine Nui*, Maroe   68.84.69
- *Relais Mahana*, Parea, B.P. 30   68.81.54
- *Tarapa Motel*, Maeva   68.81.23

Addresses for rooms in private homes are available at the Office of Tourism.

Restaurants

- *Fare Haapua* (snackbar), Fare, Huahine; proprietors Mr and Mrs Guy Flohr, Fare, Huahine.
- *Chez Mama Peni* (café-restaurant), on the seafront at Fare, Huahine.

Excursions

There are roads all around Huahine Iti and most of Huahine Nui. Towards Parea, the road runs along the coast and through vanilla plantations in the mountains. After Fitii there is a site from which one can admire or

one side Maroe Bay and on the other Bourayne port. A 100m-long bridge joins the two islands.

On Huahine Iti the road runs along the lagoon and goes through the villages of Maroe, Tefarerii and Parea. There are beautiful white sand beaches on Tiva and Haapu peninsulas. Towards the airport, the road runs beside Maeva Lake. A little before the village of Maeva, it runs beside an important archaeological site with several *marae*; amongst these, the famous Maununu *marae*. The old, picturesque village on stilts was built at the foot of Maua Tapu, the sacred mountain (429m). The road ends at Faie but a path reaches the viewpoint between Fitii and Parea. Another path runs along the coast, crossing the islet between the ocean and Lake Maeva, through coconut groves and melon plantations, until it reaches the airport and Fare.

By boat, the island tour offers the following sights: the west coast after Bali Hai Hotel, passing by the Bays of Haapu, Parea, Tefarerii, Maroe and Bourayne Port; visits to Anini *marae* and Avea beach; excursions to the *motu* of Araa and Topatii.

Bora Bora

Bora Bora lies 270 km northwest of Tahiti. The main island is surrounded by a barrier reef and several islets. There is only one pass that can be used to cross into the lagoon and the airport is built on a *motu*. Bora Bora covers 38 km^2 and its highest peak is Mount Otemanu .

Population

There are 3,240 inhabitants on the island. The principal village is Vaitape, with the administrator's residence, the post office, police station, surgery and port.

Access

By plane: three to five Air Polynesia flights a day between Tahiti and Bora Bora; either a 70 minute flight, stopping at Huahine and Raiatea; or 50 minute flight without stopovers.

By boat: three ferries service Bora Bora, leaving Tahiti once a week: *Temehani II*, *Taporo IV* and *Raromatai Ferry*.

Accommodation

- *Club Med Bora Bora*, B.P. 575, Vaitape	67.72.57
- *Hotel Bora Bora*, B.P. 1015	67.70.28
- *Hotel Oa-Oa*, B.P. 10, Vaitape	67.70.84
- *Hotel Moana Beach*, B.P. 156	67.73.73
- *Ibis Bora Bora*, B.P. 252	67.71.16
- *Marina Hotel*, B.P. 1366, Papeete	42.95.01
- *Matira Hotel*, B.P. 31	67.70.46
- *Revatua Club*, B.P. 159	67.71.67
- *Sofitel Marara*, B.P. 6	67.70.46
- *Yacht Club*, B.P. 17	67.70.69

This hotel was opened by Dino de Laurentis after the making of his film *Hurricane*.

- *Hotel Miri Miri*, Motu Paahi, B.P. 74	42.70.47
- *Hotel Royal Bora Bora*, B.P. 202	67.70.54

other rental accommodation

- *Bora Bora Bungalows*, Vaitape, B.P. 98	42.58.37
- *Bungalows Are*, Matira	67.70.73
- *Chez Aimé*, Mare	
- *Chez Fredo*, Vaitape	67.70.31
- *Chez Nono*, B.P. 12	67.71.38
- *Fare Lati*, B.P. 17	67.70.69
- *Fare Toopua*, B.P. 87	67.70.62

Rent-a-Car

- *Otemanu Rent-a-Car*, Vaitape	67.70.94
- *Polycar*	67.71.10
- *Rent-a-Car*, Vaitape	67.70.03

Rent-a-Boat

- *Moana Adventure Tours* (owner Erwin Christian) can offer you: a glass-bottom boat, excursions on the reef, picnics on an island, water-skiing, diving.

| - *Marina Excursions* | 67.70.97 |
| - *Bora Bora Aquarium* | 67.70.53 |

Things To Do

All sorts of nautical sports are practised: canoe and speedboat excursions, deepwater diving, night-fishing in the lagoon, shell collecting. A traditional stone-fishing excursion can be organized by the chief of Vaitape village, upon request.

Water sports:

| - *Calypso Club*, Hotel Marara | 67.70.46 |
| - *Moana Adventure Tours* (Erwin Christian), Hotel Bora Bora | 67.70.53 |

The island tour covers 32 kilometres of road beside the lagoon. Visit the tomb of French navigator Alain Gerbault in Vaitape on the site of an ancient *marae*.

Mountain climbing is possible on Mt. Pahia (661 m). The climb takes three hours. Visit Motu-Toopua and Motu-Tapu Islands, tour the island by boat (two to four hours) and see the Taianapa *marae* near Faanui village (km 26).

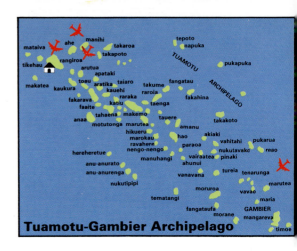

Tuamotu-Gambier Archipelago

Maupiti

Maupiti lies 37 km west of Bora Bora, has a total circumference of 9.6 km with a surface of 25 km². Surrounded by a barrier reef, its highest point reaches 372 m.

Population

800 inhabitants. There used to be 9 administrative centers; only two remain today - Vaiea and Farauru. The port, school, surgery and town hall are at Farauru.

Access

By plane: three weekly Air Polynesia flights between Tahiti and Maupiti lasting 2 hr 10 min, stopping at Raiatea and Bora Bora.

By boat: Taporo I leaves Raiatea Tuesdays   42.63.93

Accommodation

As there are no tourist hotels in Maupiti, accommodations must be made in private homes.

- *Chez Teha Teupoohuitua*, Farauru
- *Chez Teroro Raioho*, Farauru
- *Chez Tinorua Anua*, Maupiti
- *Hotel Auira*   67.80.01
- *Pension Tavaearii*, Motu Tiapaa

Excursions

There is a new road around the island, but it is well worth taking the old coastal path, starting from Vaiea village, which takes about three hours. On Pae'oa *motu* the oldest archaeological site in the Leeward Islands can be visited. There are also *marae* platforms, stone walls and dolmens to be seen on the island, with white sand beaches and islets to visit.

Local Crafts

Maupiti was well known for its crafts in stone and wood. Today the local craft is mainly mother-of-pearl fish-hooks. There are seven different kinds of mother-of-pearl, used for the seven kinds of fish-hook — one for each kind of fishing. These are still used today.

Tuamotu Archipelago

The Tuamotu archipelago is the largest in French Polynesia, formed by 84 islands that lie along a strip 2,300 km long and 400 to 500 km wide. The total land surface is 922 km², spread out over 20,000 km² of ocean. The principal island is Rangiroa. With the exception of Makatea, all the islands are low and of coral origin .

Population

The Tuamotu Islands are not densely populated; only 41 of the 84 islands are inhabited. The population is

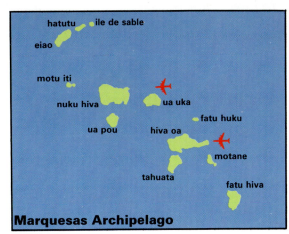

Marquesas Archipelago

11,800, 5% of the total population of French Polynesia. The largest number live in Rangiroa: 1,670 inhabitants.

Access

By plane: Air Polynesia flies to eight atolls in the Tuamotu; there are flights to Rangiroa (65 min.) six days a week (except Tuesdays). Wednesdays, Fridays and Sundays connections with Manihi; Fridays only, connections with Tikehau; once a week, on Friday, a flight from Papeete to Kaukura, Apataki, Fakarava, Takapoto returning the same day; weekly flights to Anaa and Makemo; and weekly (Friday) connections with Mataiva.

For further information contact Air Tahiti, 43.39.39.

By boat: several ferries service the Tuamotu. They are:
- *L'Allura Nui II*, Motu Uta B.P. 1291   43.76.17
- *Le Manava I* (SEPNA), B.P. 1291   43.76.17
- *Maina Nui* (Sté Utahia), Bd. Pomare, B.P. 635 42.98.46
- *Mata Riva* (SPM), B.P. 9274   43.71.09
- *Mairoa Nui* (A. Tang), Ave. Paraita, B.P. 1187 42.91.69
- *Ruahatu* (CNIM), Rue Colette, B.P. 2516   43.86.82

All necessary information may be obtained by contacting the companies and their operators.

There are atomic centers in Mururoa and Fangataufa, and a C.E.P. base in Hao. These atolls have ports and airports but, being military bases, access is forbidden to unauthorized civilians.

Accommodation

On Rangiroa:
- *Bouteille à la Mer*, B.P. 17, Avatoru   334 at Rangiroa
- *Chez Giornne*   358 at Rangiroa
- *Chez Jimmy*, B.P. 597, Papeete   42.88.44
- *Chez Marie*   394-392 at Rangiroa
- *Chez Mata*   378 at Rangiroa
- *Chez Nanua*   388 at Rangiroa
- *Kia Ora Rangiroa*, B.P. 706, Papeete   42.56.72
- *Rangiroa Village*, B.P. 8, Avato   383 at Rangiroa
- *Village Sans Soucie*, Mahuta   42.48.33

On Manihi:
- *Kaina Village Hotel*, B.P.2460   42.75.53

Pensions:
- *Chez Mrs. Estall*
- *Chez Mrs. Fareea*, Motu Topiheio

Other atolls:

Fakarava:	*Chez Danilou*	
Kaukua:	*Chez Claire*	
	Hotel Ismure Village	42.61.55
Mataiva:	*Chez Moise Tetua*	
Takaroa:	*Chez Temu*, Teavaroa	
Takaputo:	*Chez Mahei*, Tefahatepatere	
Tikehau:	*Chez Natua Arai*, *Chez Faahei*	

Gambier Archipelago

The Gambier Islands are different from the Tuamotu: they include four high islands and a few atolls. They lie to the south of the Tuamotu Archipelago. The principal

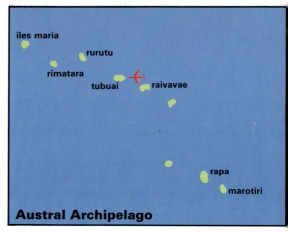

Austral Archipelago

island, Mangareva, reaches its highest point at 435 m. The population is not numerous: some 600 inhabitants in Rikitea, the capital. Air Polynesia has two monthly flights from Papeete. Ferries call from time to time and the C.E.P. has built a landing strip, which is used by air companies upon request. Agriculture, the copra industry, fishing and pearl culture are the main livelihoods of the inhabitants.

Marquesas Archipelago

The Marquesas lie 1,500 km northeast of Tahiti. Forming two groups, its 14 islands cover 1,275 km². The two groups are: the north, Nuku Hiva, Ua Uka and Ua Pou; the south, Hiva Oa, Tahuata and Fatu Hiva. They are high, craggy islands: their peaks rise to over 1,000 m and their coasts are not protected by barrier reefs.

Population

Only six islands are inhabited. The total population of 6,500 inhabitants increases by 5% per year. All the villages are in the valleys. Taiohae, the capital, is on Nuku Hiva, with schools, hospital, bishopric and port.

Access

By plane: The islands Nuku Hiva, Hiva Oa, Ua Uka and Ua Pou connect with Papeete several times a week via Air Tahiti (43.39.39).

By boat: Several ferries call regularly:

- *Ararao* makes a 20 to 25-day round trip   42.62.40

- *Tamari Tuamotu*   42.95.07
- *Taporo V* leaves Papeete every two weeks on no fixed date. The trip takes four days.   42.63.93

With no fixed schedule, there are ferries that link the several islands, but the service is not guaranteed.

Accommodation

- Atuona village (Hiva Oa): *Jean Saucourt* and the *mayor* offer rooms for rent.
- Puamau (Hiva Oa): *Bernard Heitaa* and *Mohi Tanoa* can both offer rooms.
- Hane village (Ua Uka): *Vii Fournier* has accommodation.
- Vaipaee village (Ua Uka): *Mme Miriama Fournier*, *Mme Joseph Lichtle* and *Mme Laura Raioha* have rooms to rent.
- Taiohae village (Nuku Hiva). *Becfin* restaurant has two bungalows; chez *Mate and Fetu*; three bungalows at the *Keikahanui Inn*; seven rooms at the *Moana Nui* hotel; six bungalows at *Moetai Village*.
- Vaitahu village (Tahuata): *Naani Barsinas* can offer a three-roomed house. Boat trips possible and horses to rent.
- Omoa village (Fatu Hiva): *Joseph Tetuanui*, *François Peter*, *Kehu Kania* and *Tehau Gilmore* each have houses to rent.

Excursions

There are no organized excursions in the Marquesas, but it is always possible to hire a horse, as there are a few mountain paths.

To visit: Gauguin's tomb (he died in 1903) in Atuona cemetry, on Hiva Oa. See also Jacques Brel's tomb.
- Archeological remains on Fatu Hiva, especially a *paepae* in Omoa.
- Virgin Bay, Hanavave, Fatu Hiva.
- Traitor's Bay, Atuona and Hanaiapa Bay, Hiva Oa.
- Archeological remains on Hiva Oa: *meae* and *paepae*, platforms on which the *tiki* stood. The Teii-pona *meae* were famous because of the height of their *tiki*. The highest one is at Takaiki: 3.50m.
- Taiohae Bay must be seen on Nuku Hiva.

Austral Archipelago

The Austral archipelago, 600 km south of Tahiti, includes five high islands (Tubuai, Rimatara, Rurutu, Raivavae and Rapa) and two atolls (Hull and Bass). The high islands are of volcanic origin and not very high (100-200 m), except Rapa (highest point: 1,460 m). Rapa is also the island farthest south. Tubuai is a circular island, surrounded by a barrier reef. There is only one pass that can be used, in the northeast near Mataura village. The population is 1,750. The principal villages are: Mataura in the north, Huahine in the interior, Mahu in the south and Taahuaia in the northeast. Climatically, the Austral archipelago is colder than the rest of French Polynesia, especially during the cold season, from May to October.

Population
The total population is 6,300. Five of the islands are inhabited. Rapa has the largest concentration of inhabitants, but Mataura, on Tubuai, is the capital, with the administrative centers, schools and hospital.

Access
By plane: there are airports at Tubuai and Rurutu. Air Tahiti has two flights a week, Fridays and Saturdays, to both islands.
By boat: *Tuhaapae II* leaves Papeete once or twice a month for the Austral Islands (Rimatara, Rurutu, Tubuai, Raivavae); ferries only call every two months at Rapa. 42.93.67

Accommodation
Tubai:
- *Mme Caroline Tetuaearo* lets five comfortable bungalows in Mataura.
- *M. Aumera* lets four bungalows 1 km from Mataura.
- *M. and Mme Tenepau* rent two small houses.
- the *Hermitage Sainte Hélène*, belonging to *Noel Ilari*, has several comfortable bungalows, near Mahu village. Car hire and boats for deep-sea fishing — contact the mayor of Mataura
Bicycles, mopeds and horses for hire — *M. Ato*.
Trips on the lagoon — *M. Paipi*.
Rurutu:
- *Rurutu Village*, Papeete 42.93.85

The photographers of Tahiti and its islands include:
Mike Hosken, who made the major photographic contribution in the
updating of the new edition.
Michel Folco: pages 10, 42, 66, 73, 76-77, 98-99, 103, 116, 118.
Claude Rives: pages 16-17, 18-19, 56, 95, 106, 108-109.
Bernard Hermann: pages 8-9, 55, 127.
Others are by M. Maitrot of Air Tahiti (pages 9, 125);
M. Moisnard (pages 100-101); R. Bagnis (page 102);
Charles Pinson (104); Pacifilm (page 117).

Printed in Singapore